Foreword by Dr. Georgia Purdom

ENVIRONMENT

SEX

EQUALITY

LIFE

Quick
Answers to
Social
Issues

BRYAN OSBORNE

First printing: March 2020

Second printing: December 2020

Master Books®, P.O. Box 726, Green Forest, AR 72638

Master Books® is a division of the New Leaf Publishing Group, Inc.

ISBN: 978-1-68344-202-8
ISBN: 978-1-61458-735-4 (digital)

Library of Congress Number: 2019956168

Cover by Diana Bogardus

Unless otherwise noted, Bible quotations are from the English Standard Version (ESV).
ESV — Scripture quotations are from the ESV® Bible (The Holy Bible, English Standard Version®), copyright © 2001 by Crossway, a publishing ministry of Good News Publishers. Used by permission. All rights reserved.

NASB — Scripture taken from the NEW AMERICAN STANDARD BIBLE®, Copyright © 1960, 1962, 1963, 1968, 1971, 1972, 1973, 1975, 1977, 1995 by The Lockman Foundation. Used by permission.

NIV — Scriptures taken from the Holy Bible, New International Version®, NIV®. Copyright © 1973, 1978, 1984, 2011 by Biblica, Inc.™ Used by permission of Zondervan. All rights reserved worldwide.

Please consider requesting that a copy of this volume be purchased by your local library system.

Printed in China

Please visit our website for other great titles: www.masterbooks.com

For information regarding author interviews, contact the publicity department at (870) 438-5288.

Photo and Illustration Credits:

Unless otherwise noted, all images are from istock.com
Wikimedia Commons: pg. 33, pg. 89
Images from Wikimedia Commons are used under the CC0 1.0, CC BY-SA 2.0 DE, CC-BY-SA-3.0 license or the GNU Free Documentation License, Version 1.3.
Answers in Genesis: p 73

Master Books®
A Division of New Leaf Publishing Group
www.masterbooks.com

Dedication

First and foremost, all glory goes to my God, Creator, and Savior. This book is evidence of His grace, divine intervention, and delight to use the foolish things of this world to shame the wise (1 Corinthians 1:27).

Part of His immeasurable grace to me is constantly displayed in the gift of my beautiful bride. Marla, you are my greatest earthly blessing, my best friend, an incredible mother, and I'm eternally thankful that you are my partner in all things life and ministry (Proverbs 18:22)!

I also must confess that the image of my gorgeous children, Ian and Macie, was ever present in my mind as I wrote this book. Daddy loves you more than you can know and my greatest desire for you is to know, enjoy, and glorify Christ! I hope this book will help you do just that.

It's my prayer that God will use this book as a tool for His glory in equipping the saints to valiantly stand on God's Word, boldly defend their faith, and lovingly share the good news of Jesus Christ to a lost, confused, and dying world!

Galatians 2:20

About the Author

Bryan Osborne is passionate about equipping believers with the truth of God's Word to boldly defend the faith and proclaim the gospel! As an expert in the use of exciting, apologetics-based evangelism and chronological Bible teaching, this former athlete connects with audiences at a real-world level while demonstrating real evidence confirms the truth of the Bible.

After graduating from Bryan College with a BA in Biblical Studies, and minors in Christian Education and Greek, he later received his Master's degree in Education from Lee University. For 13 years Bryan boldly and enthusiastically taught Bible history in a public school in Tennessee, and for over 20 years he has helped Christians in the local church to know and defend their faith.

He now speaks at conferences and in churches for Answers in Genesis. An in-demand speaker, he travels across the US and around the world encouraging, challenging, and equipping believers to stand on biblical authority. He also serves as a writer and curriculum specialist within the ministry.

Bryan's giftedness as a communicator, love of the gospel, and his passion for revealing biblical truth is both obvious and contagious. You will love his practical, engaging style that equips believers with the answers they need to stand fast on God's Word, champion the faith, and courageously declare the gospel of Jesus Christ!

Foreword

As the chair of the Editorial Review Board here at Answers in Genesis, I lead a team that ensures everything Answers in Genesis produces is accurate, top-quality, and within our ministry's mission, purpose, and beliefs. I therefore had the pleasure of reading and reviewing Bryan's newest book, the volume you are holding today.

Our culture has been experiencing a dramatic social upheaval since the 1960s and the beginning of the sexual revolution. But it seems this upheaval has become even more violent and unrelenting within the last few years. What was unthinkable even a decade ago is now commonplace and splashed all over the news headlines (and if you haven't swallowed it hook, line, and sinker, you're considered an old-fashioned bigot not fit for society). And yet so many of these issues fly in the face of biblical truth. How should Christians think? How should we engage with the culture, effectively sharing biblical truth and pointing everyone towards the life-changing message of the gospel?

That's why *Quick Answers to Social Issues* is so valuable. In his easy-to-read style, Bryan lays a solid, proper foundation to begin the discussion. He rightly shows the true nature of the discussion (more of a war, really!) — it's a battle over worldviews and, ultimately, foundations. And there are only two options: man's word or God's Word. We either start with man's arbitrary and fallible opinions and ideas, or we start with the infallible Word of the infallible God. There is no other option! It's vital we understand this truth before we get into discussions about hot-button issues.

In this book, Bryan doesn't shy away from any of the "tough questions," even though many in our culture say he is not qualified or able to address them because of his gender or ethnic background. God's Word is sufficient for everyone to give an answer for the hope we have (1 Peter 3:15), regardless of whether they are male or female, an ethnic minority or majority, or any other factor. God's Word is our sword, able to be wielded by all believers, at all times, in all cultures. And he rightly applies God's Word to many of the most contentious issues facing our culture today.

Bryan deals with complex issues in a very straightforward way, not getting lost in complexities, details, or "rabbit trails" — in essence, he delivers exactly what he promises with the title *Quick Answers*. This book is a great exercise in how to think — once you understand foundational principles, you can apply them to the complexities, details, or other issues that may arise someday in the future.

After finishing this book, I know you will feel more equipped to address the pervasive lies of our culture. Take what you learn and apply it by talking to others, thinking critically about what you hear from the media and others, and teaching those around you to also think biblically.

—Dr. Georgia Purdom
Director of Educational Content, Speaker, and Author

LIFE

Introduction

"You fool"

"You fool," said my friend and colleague with lighthearted laughter when I shared the idea of this book. I knew exactly what he meant. To publicly address any one of these issues today, even in much of the church, is to tread on dangerous waters — much less all the topics covered in this book! But these are the waters Christians swim in today, whether we like it or not.

No doubt, the subjects we'll cover are "hot button" issues, and they are for a reason. **They're part of a full-scale assault by the enemy, particularly in the West, aimed at demolishing biblical authority and Christian morality.** And the "father of lies" (John 8:44) doesn't like his schemes interfered with. In recent generations, the devil's been using the same old "Genesis 3 attack" in a unique way. When Satan said to Eve, "Did God really say?" the scheme was to get her to question, doubt, and ultimately reject what God plainly said. The method was extremely effective, and he's been employing it ever since in various ways. Recently, ideas like evolution, big bang, and millions of years have been his way of saying, "Did God really say?" He uses these ideas to attack biblical history and to undercut biblical authority in order to discredit the Bible's teaching on morality and salvation. The bottom line is, **if the Bible cannot be trusted when it speaks on history, why trust it when it speaks on morality, society, or eternity** (John 3:12)? If the Bible's beginning can't be trusted, why trust the middle or the end? Either all of the

BIBLE REF.
Genesis 3:1–7
John 8:44
John 3:12
2 Corinthians 10:5
Philippians 1:27
2 Timothy 2:24-25
1 Peter 3:15

Bible is trustworthy and authoritative, or none of it is!

The collapse of the Christian worldview in **America** and throughout the West is happening to the utter shock of Christians. Why? They've been blind to the enemy's stealth attack on biblical history and authority that has led multiple generations to abandon God's Word as their foundation. With God's Word removed, people feel empowered to redefine history, reality, society, and morality. The issues addressed in this book are the "tip of the spear" for the enemy to radically transform a once exceedingly Christianized culture.

When our culture asks the questions dealt with in this book — and our kids parrot these questions and ideas heard from schools, libraries, movies, books, music, YouTube, social media, etc. — it must be remembered they're not innocent, unintentional questions. They stem fundamentally from a rejection of biblical authority and have the agenda of remaking the culture into the enemy's image. With that in mind, it's imperative that Christians be ready to give answers to today's questions (1 Peter 3:15)! And these answers must be rooted in the Bible because, ultimately, this is a foundational battle of authority between the word of men and the Word of God.

Thus the passion and purpose of this book — to equip Christians with clear, concise biblical answers to effectively stand on God's Word and boldly proclaim the gospel of Jesus Christ on the frontlines of today's battle!

Only two?

It is often claimed that there are so many different religions, with diverse views, that it's impossible to know who's right. Taken a step further, the claim is "nobody is right." This philosophy permeates our culture, has affected the thinking of many Christians, and has a couple of major problems.

One, if someone claims that nobody is right, are they right about nobody being right? **If they are right that nobody is right, then they — being somebody — are wrong about being right. How can that be right?** The very idea is fundamentally self-refuting.

Here's the second major problem. **Foundationally, there are actually only two religions. Just two? Just two. They are God's and man's.** And these two fundamental religions could not be more different. God's religion is articulated in the tenets of Christianity rightly reasoned from the Bible, the divine revelation of the Creator God Himself. The religion of man is expressed in seemingly endless ways, with the central dogma being that man can determine truth apart from God.

Either there is a Creator God who made everything, who has revealed Himself to us in a clear way and holds everyone accountable to His revelation, or people are just rearranged pond scum who create gods in their own image to suit themselves and define truth however they see fit. In man's religion, truth is relative and manipulated by individuals. In God's religion, there is only one truth — His. God is the absolute, eternal, unchanging cornerstone of all truth that rightly defines all of reality.

BIBLE REF.
Genesis 3:5
I Chronicles 29:11–13
Psalm 119:89
Matthew 7:24–27
Luke 16:17
I Thessalonians 2:13

And no matter the issue in question — origins, morality, sexuality, significance of existence, salvation, future reality, etc. — how a person answers will ultimately come down to one of the only two religions. Do you trust the Word of God or words of men? Do you put your hope in the hands of broken, sinful, finite people (which includes yourself and your own thinking) who don't know everything, who haven't always existed, who on their own have no rationality for truth, reason, morality, or love? Or do you trust the revelation of the living God — the words of the One who is eternal, infinite, all-knowing, all-powerful, unchanging, perfect, who cannot lie, and is the very origin of love, truth, knowledge, reason, goodness, and existence?

It is from one of these two foundations that everyone must build their thinking and worldview. Either God's Word is esteemed as the highest authority and rightly submitted to in every area or is rejected and all that is left are the diverse, contradictory ideas of men, which an individual must use to create a worldview with a pseudo-authority. This actually makes the individual the ultimate authority; he becomes his own god. As will be discussed in more detail in the next chapter, there is no such thing as neutrality. Either trust God or "you will be like god" (Genesis 3:5).

The neutrality myth

One of the most pervasive cultural myths today is that people can be and should be neutral. The narrative of neutrality goes hand in hand with the current secular redefining of tolerance and belief in relativism. In essence, **the push for neutrality is based on the false assumptions of no absolute truth, beliefs don't assume an authority, and people can be unbiased.**

Of course, none of these things are true. The best way to expose the naïve notion of neutrality is by going to the foundation. As discussed previously, there are only two fundamental religions, only two foundational worldviews. One is established on God's Word and the other on man's. Both presume an authority; it's literally impossible not to. Someone either trusts God's Word as the ultimate authority and builds their thinking, their worldview, from there, or they reject the Bible as absolute and instead form their opinions, their worldview, from the ideas of men. Everyone makes a choice, whether they realize it or not, to submit and live according to one or the other.

This is why the Bible says, "The mind set on the flesh is hostile toward God" (Romans 8:7; NASB) and "friendship with the world is hostility toward God" (James 4:4; NASB). We realize Jesus meant what He said in Matthew 12:30 (NASB), "He who is **not with** Me is **against** Me; and he who does **not gather** with Me **scatters.**" The Bible is unequivocal — no one can be neutral. Therefore, the claim that neutrality is possible is anti-biblical

BIBLE REF.
Jeremiah 23:29
Matthew 12:30
Romans 8:7
2 Timothy 3:16
James 4:4
Hebrews 4:12
2 Peter 1:20–21

and consequently not neutral.

It must be recognized that no matter the issue, from origins to abortion, it's ultimately a battle of authority. Either God's Word or man's is preeminent. So, how should a Christian respond when debating whatever subject and they're asked to abandon the Bible in favor of "neutral ground"? Absolutely not! Why? Because there is no "neutral ground"! Neutrality is biblically impossible. Every issue comes down to whose word is supreme. **If the believer agrees that the Bible is not needed for truth on any issue, by default they've conceded that man's word is the ultimate authority! "Neutral ground" is actually man's ground since it opposes biblical authority.**

Here's a helpful analogy based on the biblical portrayal of God's Word as a sword. Imagine you're a knight, centuries ago, facing down an opposing knight. As you both draw your swords to commence battle, the opposing knight says, "I don't believe in your sword, get rid of it!" You could concede, discard your sword, and get skewered. Or a better option — use your sword and its reality will become evident!

Two things to remember when someone asks you to be neutral — they're not, and you can't be. And you shouldn't pretend to be. The Bible is our sword, our authority, and every conflict we face today is a battle over authority. You cannot defend biblical authority by abandoning biblical authority! Don't fall for the lie of neutrality — use your sword to the glory of God!

Be "tolerant" or else

Tolerance is a single word encompassing the central creed of today's enlightened secular culture. In a society where everyone creates their own truth and autonomy paraded through personal expression is worshiped, intolerance is the supreme evil.

To more fully understand this sacred secular doctrine, the popular contemporary understanding of tolerance must be contrasted to its traditional definition. Its classical meaning, found in most dictionaries, is essentially the practice of tolerating the existence of ideas or behaviors that one disagrees with. For those swept up in today's progressive indoctrination, this definition doesn't go far enough, nor is "tolerance" a two-way street.

The current secular manifestation of tolerance demands so much more than a willingness to accept the existence of ideas contrary to one's own. One must not only endure, but also *celebrate* contrary ideas and *empower* those who hold them. But this superficially assumes relativism — no absolutes — and the equivalence of various, contradicting truth claims. The secularist is blindly trusting that belief in absolute truth is absolutely wrong, a declaration ironically impossible within their worldview.

In theory, if they believed their own definition of tolerance, they would celebrate, encourage, and empower those who hold beliefs different than their own. As previously mentioned, the secularist's version of tolerance isn't a two-way street. It's only their ideas that require celebratory approval. They have

BIBLE REF.
Genesis 3
2 Chronicles 36:16
Proverbs 28:4
Matthew 10:32
Romans 1:18–32
Ephesisans 5:11
1 John 4:15

no desire or inclination to reciprocate this practice to any other view. There's an outright refusal by secularists to consistently apply and practice their own ultimate standard of tolerance.

Scaling the heights of hypocrisy, the secularist arbitrarily and strategically redefines tolerance, requires agreement, demands compliance, and then is bigotedly intolerant — by the old or new definition — toward anyone with an opposing view. Anyone who dares defy the progressive mantra is labeled hateful, bigoted, and intolerant.

The secularists' "altar call" proclaims that if you don't already hold to today's "open-minded" values, now's the time to "repent and believe" — or else. **You will comply or you won't be tolerated. Ironically, those who champion tolerance as supreme unveil themselves as fantastically intolerant.**

The secularist only **"superficially** assumes...no absolutes." He does believe in absolutes in his heart of hearts, just not God's. **He actually elevates his own thoughts and beliefs to the level of absolute truth.** That's why the secularist is so bigoted and intolerant toward those who disagree. You either agree with what is "unequivocally right" or suffer the fate of all nonbelievers. In his mind, whether he recognizes it or not, his ideas — his "word" — has become the standard. This revelation exposes the foundational battle that traces its roots all the way back to Genesis 3. Either God's the authority in your life or you are. No one can serve two masters; both won't be tolerated.

In reality, Christianity is supremely tolerant. How? All are sinners who need a Savior, and anyone who repents and trusts in Christ alone will be saved. The door is open to all. It doesn't get more tolerant than that.

The Genesis connection

"What do today's social issues have to do with Genesis?" Along with the authority issue addressed earlier, the history of Genesis 1–11 is literally the foundation for every biblical doctrine either directly or indirectly. If you destroy the foundation, the doctrines resting on that foundation collapse.

In Genesis, we see the all-powerful Creator make a perfect creation with no death, disease, or bloodshed. As the crowning jewel of His creation, God makes man, male and female, in His image. **This history** explains the reality of only two genders. Also, it's why every person — no matter their age, appearance, location, ability, disability — has inherent and indelible value and dignity. Because all people descend from those first two image bearers, **every person reflects the *Imago Dei*** (Latin meaning "image of God") from womb to tomb. Thus, Christians can authoritatively say that **abortion, euthanasia, discrimination, abuse, etc., are wrong.**

Genesis 2 recounts the creation and definition of **marriage,** the biblical institution that's foundational to society. This is how we know that marriage is between one man and one woman for life. **God made marriage, and He defines what it is.**

In the history of Genesis 3, Adam sinned, bringing death and suffering into this world just as God warned. It's clear from Genesis to Revelation that man's sin brought death, the enemy, into God's perfect creation. Because of sin, all of creation was corrupted (Romans 8:22). **This history explains the beauty in the world, remnants of God's original flawless creation, and**

BIBLE REF.
Genesis 1–11
Genesis 2
Romans 5:12–17
Romans 8:22
I Corinthians 15:21–22

the ugly reality of death, suffering, brokenness and disease, all resulting from the fall.[1]

Noah's Flood in Genesis 6–9 explains the majority of the fossil record, and the event of the Tower of Babel, Genesis 10–11, explains the origins of languages and people groups. This history testifies to the truth that all people trace their family tree back to Adam and Eve. So, biologically and biblically speaking, there is only one race, the human race! Every human is equally made in God's image; therefore, racism is nonsense! And since every person descends from the first Adam who fell into sin, everyone is born a sinner. This inherited sin nature explains why all people have thoughts, desires, and proclivities that are out of step with God's original design and are in need of saving through the Last Adam, Jesus Christ.

The main point here is to recognize that **every biblical doctrine that must be used to combat the secular dogma of this age is rooted in Genesis.**

---

1 Attempting to put millions of years into the Bible always puts death before sin. And death before sin rejects the clear history of Scripture and is theologically impossible. You see, if there is death before sin, then death is not the payment for sin. And if death is not the payment for sin, then Jesus' death cannot pay our sin debt — one of many reasons the humanistic idea of millions of years is incompatible with the Bible.

How can you believe the Bible?

Many argue that "The Bible cannot be trusted because it's written by men!" Does that mean anything said or written by "men" is untrustworthy? What about textbooks used in classrooms worldwide? Can the words of the one making the argument be trusted because they're also a person? More importantly, **the Bible's clear that God is the ultimate author of Scripture** (1 Thessalonians 2:13). All of Scripture is "God-breathed" (2 Timothy 3:16; NIV); the human authors wrote as they were "moved" by the Holy Spirit (2 Peter 1:21).

The Bible is trustworthy in all that it says because it's the revelation of the one true, living God — the God who cannot lie, is all-knowing, all-powerful, everywhere existing, infinite, eternal, unchanging, good, and perfect.

If one is willing to look, confirmations of this eternal truth are everywhere. Historically, no other history is close to the veracity of the Bible's history. **The Bible has more manuscripts written closer to the original events than any other trusted historical record.** And over 20,000 archaeological discoveries have confirmed biblical history.

The Bible is extraordinarily unique, written over 1,500 years, on three different continents, in multiple languages, by 40-plus authors from remarkably diverse backgrounds. **The fact that the Bible is utterly cohesive and focused on the singular theme of Christ from beginning to end is tremendous testimony of its supernatural nature.**

BIBLE REF.
2 Samuel 22:31
Psalm 12:6
Proverbs 30:5
Matthew 7:24–27
Ephesians 6:17
1 Thessalonians 2:13
2 Timothy 3:16
2 Peter 1:21

It's often asserted that science has disproved the Bible. Answers in Genesis has thousands of resources demonstrating the exact opposite! Real science repeatedly confirms the Bible and constantly unveils the faulty worldview bias leading secular scientists to erroneous conclusions about unseen history. My previous book, *Quick Answers to Tough Questions*, concisely deals with many of these issues.[1]

Fulfilled prophecy puts the Bible in a supernatural league all its own. The Bible contains hundreds of fulfilled prophecies of future events, often hundreds of years before they occur, with 100% accuracy, which demands divinity.

A forceful demonstration of the Bible's unrivaled truthfulness is that only the biblical worldview can self-consistently make sense of all reality without contradicting itself. The attributes and actions of the biblical God alone provide the only rational reason for the existence of the material world and non-material things like the laws of logic, laws of nature, and absolute morality — things that cannot be seen, tasted, or touched but are absolutely real. These immaterial realities must be true for us to live, think, and function but make no sense without the biblical God and humans made in His image.

Without the biblical worldview being true, you wouldn't be able to coherently ask the initial question! **Since only the Bible can consistently explain knowledge, logic, truth, and our ability to use them, the very ability to ask is confirmation of the exclusivity of biblical truth!**[2]

---

1 There are also numerous articles, videos, and resources on our website, answersingenesis.org, that powerfully demonstrate the scientific confirmation of biblical history.

2 For more on this, see Jason Lisle's book, *The Ultimate Proof of Creation* (Green Forest, AR: Master Books, 2009).

Life Issues

What's the biblical response to abortion?

There are many powerful arguments against pro-abortionist claims, some of which will be presented later. If these arguments are rooted in anything less than the rock of God's Word, all that's actually happening is a comparison of one person's ideas to another.

With this in mind, there are at least three fundamental questions concerning abortion that must be biblically addressed: When does life begin? What is the entity in the mother's womb? What is its value? A quick survey of Scripture reveals that God has authoritatively addressed each of these issues.

> *For you formed my inward parts;*
> *you knitted me together in my mother's womb.*
> *I praise you, for I am fearfully and wonderfully made.*
> *Wonderful are your works;*
> *my soul knows it very well.*
> *My frame was not hidden from you,*
> *when I was being made in secret,*
> *intricately woven in the depths of the earth.*
> *Your eyes saw my unformed substance;*
> *in your book were written, every one of them,*
> *the days that were formed for me,*
> *when as yet there was none of them.*
> *(Psalm 139:13–16)*

BIBLE REF.
Genesis 9:6
Exodus 20:13
Psalm 139:13–16
Exodus 21:22–24
Job 31:15
Jeremiah 1:5, 3:15
Isaiah 49:1–5
Luke 1:39–44

Notice all the personal pronouns used by the Psalmist to describe God's interaction with him before his birth. God is unmistakably engaging a person, a human being, inside the mother's womb. **Every single time the Bible speaks of the unborn, they're referenced as a person, a living human being** (Exodus 21:22–24; Job 31:15; Jeremiah 1:5; Isaiah 49:1–5; Luke 1:39–44).

The Psalmist declares that not only did God form and know him in the womb, God knew all the days and details of his life before they began! This sentiment is echoed throughout Scripture. In Jeremiah 1:5, God tells Jeremiah, "Before I formed you in the womb **I knew you.**" So not only does life begin at fertilization, but each person is known in the mind of God from eternity past!

What's the value of every person, known and formed by God, during their stay in the womb? Biblically, the value and personhood of an individual inside of the womb is never differentiated from someone outside. **As established by Genesis 1:27, every person, no matter their age — one second to one hundred — or location — in the womb or on the moon — is made in God's image.** Every human is stamped with the *Imago Dei* and thus has intrinsic, permanent, God-appointed value and dignity. Human life is so unique and precious, if someone purposely takes the life of a human being, the cost is their life. God declares in Genesis 9:6, *Whoever sheds human blood, by humans shall their blood be shed; for in the image of God has God made mankind (NIV).* **God's Word is clear. What exists in the mother's womb is a person made in the image of God, known by their maker before fertilization. Purposely taking that life at any point is murder.** God, the giver and sustainer of life, has not left us guessing.

Isn't abortion a woman's legal right and choice?

It's often said that abortion is a complicated issue. It's really not. Now the circumstances surrounding abortion can be horrendously complex, but not abortion itself. If the unborn isn't a person, abortion is a non-issue. But since it's known conclusively from God's Word that the unborn is a person, abortion is murder. **With the beginning and value of life definitively defined by the author of life Himself, answering the plethora of pro-abortion (pro-choice) arguments is remarkably easy** (Psalm 139:13–16; Jeremiah 1:5).

Fetus,
9 weeks

BIBLE REF.
Exodus 20:13
Leviticus 24:17
Psalm 139:13–16
Jeremiah 1:5; 31:15
Romans 14:11–12

Abortion is a woman's right and choice!

Nowhere in the Bible or in civilized legal codes around the world does a man or woman have the legitimate "right" to "choose" to murder an innocent human being, no matter where they reside.

A woman can do what she wants with her body!

The Bible vehemently denounces this. God, the author and sustainer of life, has given clear instructions on what humans can and cannot do with their bodies. **No one has total autonomy regarding their body because everyone's accountable to God for how they use the gift of their lives and bodies in accordance to His Word.** Additionally and ironically, many man-made laws limit what people, women included, can do with their bodies. One example is that public nudity in America is illegal. Thank goodness!

Here's the other major issue — in the mother's womb lives an entirely different person who's not part of the mother's body! **The Bible always addresses the womb-residing baby as a distinct and unique person. Biology and genetics bear this out. Consider that roughly half of the babies living in their mother's wombs are males. Also recognize that each baby in the womb represents a unique combination of genetic information never before seen and never to be seen again.**

Abortion is legal!

The word or idea of abortion appears **nowhere** in America's constitution. It was legalized in 1973 when a majority of supreme court justices interpreted the Constitution in a particular way. **But being legal does not make something right.** For many years it was legal to own slaves in America and illegal for them or women to vote. **Pretty much everything Hitler did in Nazi Germany was legal. Anybody want to reasonably argue that Hitler was morally right?**

As an aside, in the culturally dominate worldview of secularism, why would it matter if a woman (or anyone else) had their "rights" stripped away and their bodies abused? In evolution, women, like everyone else, are just bags of random chemical reactions. Who cares what one set of chemical reactions does to another? And if life is all about survival of the fittest, it makes perfect sense for males who are generally stronger to dominate females who are generally weaker. If there's no God, morality is utterly relative and "might makes right." The idea that women are equivalent to men in value is only consistently found in the Christian worldview, starting way back in Genesis where both are made in God's image.

Isn't it just a fetus, unviable outside the womb?

Again, if the Christian engages these questions with a biblical worldview, they're not that hard.

"It's just a fetus or a clump of cells."

As seen in the previous chapter, this is biblically impossible. **What's in the mother's womb? A baby, a human being, a person made in God's image. Who says? God does.** And since He's omniscient and the Creator of life, He authoritatively knows.

"But it's unviable outside the womb."

True, the unborn baby cannot survive on its own out of the womb. Neither can the newborn carried full term. Would it be okay to kill a newborn baby because they can't survive on their own? How about a toddler? They need just as much help. What about a teenager? Some parents are convinced their teens would die on their own! And if those same adults were honest, most adults need help surviving in life. The point? **Autonomous survival, viability, and even one's contribution to society doesn't establish humanity or value. God determined the significance of every person when He made them in His image.**

"What if it's conceived in rape or incest?"

Although abortion itself isn't complicated, sometimes the circumstances around it are heinous and appallingly complex. The grief, brokenness, and emotional stress of the victim of such horrific crimes are real and scream for justice. They also demand the utmost love, care, and wisdom from trustworthy

BIBLE REF.
Genesis 1:27
Deuteronomy 22:25, 24:16
Ezekiel 18:4, 20
John 15:13

people. However, the reality of the pain of the victim does not change the reality of the person in the womb. A unique individual, adorned with God's image, innocent of the events leading to their existence, dwells in the mother's womb (Genesis 1:27). Neither the circumstances of conception, nor the moral bankruptcy of the father, nullify the humanity of the baby in the womb. **In no way would justice be served by killing the unborn child for the crimes of the father. Instead, punish the rapist.**

It's worth noting that the percentage of abortions related to rape, incest, or endangerment to the mother's life (covered next) is less than 1% of all abortions.

"What if the mother's life is endangered?"

This is another example of the consequences of living in a broken, cursed creation. There are extremely rare situations when pregnancy, or complications during pregnancy, genuinely puts the mother's life at risk, the child's life at risk, or both. In these scenarios, the primary goal is to save both lives, as both are made in God's image. If that's not possible, everything should be done to save the mother's life. If the child tragically dies during the process of saving the mother's life, it is a heart-wrenching consequence of living in a fallen, sin-cursed world. It's also justifiably possible that the mother could choose to risk her life to save her child's life. Obviously, the life and health of both is preferred. Where a choice must be made, there is no greater love than to lay down one's life for another, and what a powerful display of the gospel.

Shouldn't people have the right to die?

Suffering and death are two unavoidable realities every human regrettably faces. Why? Genesis 3. Death and the curse entered this world because of Adam's sin just as God warned (Genesis 2:17). Adam's sin nature was passed on to all of humanity, resulting in everyone being born a sinner by nature and consequently by choice (Romans 3:23). Thus, the plague of death was spread to all (Romans 5:12, 6:23; Hebrews 9:27).

What's the appropriate response when suffering and death come calling? Enter the issue of euthanasia, the intentional ending of a life to relieve pain and suffering. Some call it "mercy killing"; the Bible calls it murder. Acceptance of this practice is rapidly growing, and Christians need to be ready to respond.

Euthanasia, at its core, is the desire to take something that doesn't belong to humanity. Control. A yearning to "be like God" (Genesis 3:5). The thinking is that people can't dodge the certainty of death but at least they can control its "how" and "when." This reflects the adored secular doctrine of autonomy. "It's my life, I live it on my terms, I end it on my terms." And in evolutionary, secular thinking, this makes sense. People are just highly evolved animals and if they want to die, fine. Their death really is no different than the death of a roach or fern. Actually, their death would free up resources for others to consume and enjoy. It could be argued, and some do, that those consuming too much of society's resources without adequate contribution have a duty to die.

BIBLE REF.
Genesis 3, 2:17, 9:6
Exodus 20:13
Job 14:5, 33:4
Acts 17:25, 28
Romans 3:23, 5:12–24
Romans 6:23
1 Corinthians 15:21–22
Hebrews 9:17, 27

Those are the ideas of fallen, fallible, finite men. What does the authoritative Word of God say? Humans aren't animals. Every person reflects God's image and each life is precious beyond human comprehension to God. **No one has the right to intentionally take the life, to murder, another human being. Even with "good" or "merciful" intentions. Even if the person requests death. Even if the person takes their own life. Murder is the verdict in each case.** The Bible explicitly forbids murder (Exodus 20:13), and God takes it so seriously that Genesis 9:6 basically says if you murder, you die.

Biblical bottom line: each life — even your own — belongs to God.
As sovereign Creator, He's the giver and sustainer of life (Acts 17:25, 28) and the appointer of death (Hebrews 9:17). God decides when life begins and when and how it ends (Job 14:5, 33:4). This jurisdiction is the Creator's alone. **And since He's omniscient, omnipotent, and perfect in love, mercy, goodness, and justice, His judgments are always right.**

Many biblical passages proclaim the bad news of death because of sin but then go immediately to the gospel (Romans 5:12–21, 6:23; 1 Corinthians 15:21–22)! God is the giver of life, the appointer of death, and the only source of eternal life. **Death is an enemy everyone faces. An enemy only Christ can and did defeat! One day death will die, and those found in Christ will share that victory** (1 Corinthians 15:26)!

What about cloning?

Cloning is the process in which a genetically identical copy of a gene, cell, or organism is produced. Cloning occurs in nature usually through asexual reproduction. Identical twins, the result of a splitting fertilized egg, are clones (but still completely unique individuals). The focus here is the artificial cloning of an entire organism, especially as it relates to humans.

How does cloning work in general terms? Well, remove the nucleus (storehouse of DNA) from a cell of an animal desired to be cloned. Take an egg cell (from the same type of animal), remove its nucleus and transfer the donor nucleus into the egg cell. Do some initial chemical and incubation manipulation, and if it all works out, you've got a clone. This has been done to various animals, the most famous of which is "Dolly," the clone of a six-year-old sheep that grabbed the world's attention in 1996.

Although the explanation here is simple, the actual process is extremely technical and problematic. Take Dolly for example. It took 277 eggs to produce 29 embryos to create one living sheep. **That's 276 failures out of 277 attempts! This is the normal drastic failure rate for cloning across the board that you don't usually hear about.** Not only that, Dolly died at the age of 6, which is exceptionally premature for sheep. Why? She was essentially "born" at the age of six — the age of the sheep she was cloned from.

BIBLE REF.
Genesis 1:26–28
Exodus 21:12
Isaiah 42:5
Romans 13:9–10
Luke 6:31
Ephesians 6:1–4

There are two primary purposes for cloning: to produce an identical organism, called reproductive cloning, or to make a cloned embryo to harvest stem cells, called **therapeutic cloning.**

So, are there ethical issues with human cloning? Well, if evolution were true, there shouldn't be. **If people are just highly evolved animals, no different in value to a sheep or cow, then who cares? Cloning a human, no matter how they turn out or how they are used, is no problem!** But evolution is a lie and God's Word is true, so there are serious problems.

What are some biblical problems with the reproductive cloning of humans? Most cloning attempts fail, and the "successful" ones are littered with genetic problems and die prematurely. **The process would necessitate extensive experimentation on humans and inevitably lead to the deaths of numerous people (remember, embryos are human beings) to successfully make a clone.** Neither the experimenting on nor the murder of God's unique image bearers can in any way be reconciled with the Bible. It's also worth noting that cloning a human being deliberately sets out to make an individual with no natural parents. This is completely opposed to God's created order and biblical principles (Genesis 1:26–28).

And therapeutic cloning? The whole goal is to create an embryo to be destroyed after its stem cells are collected. Human embryos are human beings. **In this scenario, human beings are being brought into existence merely for parts and are then destroyed.** That's not only a crime against humanity, it's a crime against the Author of humanity.

What's the big deal with stem cells?

A stem cell is a cell that has the unique ability of turning into many specialized cells. From the time of fertilization, stems cells are used to make all the different cell types necessary for the development of the body. In fact, all of the roughly 200 different specialized cells in the body can be derived from stem cells. As maturation continues, stem cells become less versatile and reservoirs of stem cells are produced and used for cell replenishment and repair.

Why are people so excited about stem cells? Well, because of their distinct adaptability, they have the potential to treat a whole host of diseases from diabetes to Parkinson's! Many doctors and medical researchers are saying stem cell research is one of the most exciting medical advances in our lifetime.

There are two basic types of stem cells: embryonic stem cells and adult stem cells.

Embryonic stem cells are gathered from embryos, as you likely guessed. They have the advantage of being more versatile than adult stem cells, at least in theory. **They have the disadvantages of being prone to forming tumors and, as with any transplant, being rejected by the body as a foreign tissue. It is significant to note that despite the hype,** embryonic stem cells have yet to achieve any significant clinical success. Adult stem cells can actually be gathered from any fully formed person,

BIBLE REF.
Leviticus 24:17
Jeremiah 1:4–5
Matthew 19:18
Romans 3:8, 13:9

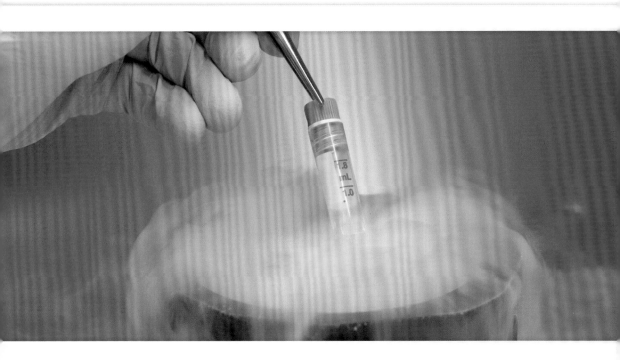

from newborn to adult, and can be found in many different tissues in the body. They do have the disadvantages of occurring in smaller numbers and being less adaptable than embryonic stem cells. **But they also have key advantages. They do not have the problem of tumor formation nor the drawback of tissue rejection as long as they come from the patient.** Many research protocols involving adult stem cells are presently ongoing. It's one of the most active arenas in medical research, with very encouraging results. Some adult stem cell therapies — those involving bone marrow transplants — have been used quite successfully for over 40 years. Dozens of diseases are currently being evaluated as potential candidates for intervention with adult stem cells.

So, what's the controversy over stem cells? It boils down to how they are obtained. Adult stem cells can be gathered from many different bodily tissues and do not put the life of the source patient at risk. What about embryonic stem cells? In order to collect them, the embryo must be "disrupted," a euphemism for killed.

As already biblically defined, life begins at fertilization, the moment a sperm unites with an egg. From that moment forward, what exists is a unique human being made in the sacred image of God (Jeremiah 1:4–5). **So, the acquisition of embryonic stem cells requires the "disruption," the murder, of a human being.** We all want to see the end of horrendous diseases, but the murder of one person to try to help another is morally and biblically indefensible.

LIFE

Equality Issues

The biblical answer to racism

The remarkable truth unseen by many, including a lot of Christians, is that only the Bible can consistently account for racism's origin, wickedness, and solution. **The root cause of racism is sin**. Period. It's been rightly said, "Racism is not a skin problem but a sin problem." And as I've had the opportunity to travel the world, I have seen this fleshed out. No matter where one goes — Japan, Malaysia, England, Africa, New Zealand, etc. — racism lifts its ugly head in various forms. Different excuses are employed: someone's from the wrong tribe, the wrong social class, they're too dark or too light, on and on the list goes. It boils down to the fact that no matter where people live, they all descend from Adam and consequently are sinners. **All people in their sinful pride can find any number of reasons to exalt themselves and belittle others.**

The biblical worldview not only explains the origin of racism but also why it is fundamentally depraved. The Bible thoroughly documents that all people descend from one man (1 Corinthians 15:45) and one woman (Genesis 3:20), and are of one blood (Acts 17:26; Malachi 2:10). This means that every person who has ever lived traces their family tree back to Adam and Eve, is made in God's image, is equal in value, and that only one biological race exists — the human race! **Racism in any form rejects the equality of every person assigned by the Creator God Himself.**

BIBLE REF.
Genesis 1:27, 3:20
Ezekiel 36:26
Malachi 2:10
1 Corinthians 15:45
Mark 12:30–31
Acts 17:26
James 2:8–9

It's important to note that if evolution were true, it would be impossible to coherently argue that racism is wrong. In the evolutionary worldview, it's logically expected that some people would be more evolved than others. That's what Darwin concluded in his book *The Descent of Man* when he said,

> At some future period... the civilized races of man will almost certainly exterminate and replace the savage races throughout the world.[1]

In Darwin's evolutionary thinking, the more advanced "civilized races" were the Caucasians, and the "savage races" were those of darker skin. Also, if evolution is true and God doesn't exist, then morality is relative and people are just animals. Why not arbitrarily hate, oppress, or kill someone or a group of people, especially if it increases your survival value? That's what Hitler did in alignment with his passionate commitment to evolution and eugenics. And again, one cannot authoritatively say that Hitler was wrong without an appeal to God, who is the absolute standard for right and wrong.

With all the commentary on racism today, there's only one real solution — the Gospel of Jesus Christ. The Bible alone establishes the equality of all people (Genesis 1:27), demands impartial love for all (Mark 12:30–31; James 2:8–9), explains the existence of racism human-wide, and illuminates racism's sole cure of a changed heart through salvation in the Last Adam (1 Corinthians 15:45; 2 Corinthians 5:17; Ezekiel 36:26)!

---

1 Charles Darwin, *The Descent of Man* (Chicago, IL: Publisher William Benton in Great Books of the Western World, 1952), p. 336.

What about "interracial" marriage?

Biblically and biologically speaking, there's no such thing! Since all people descend from Adam and Eve, there's only one biological race — a truth the science of genetics is repeatedly confirming as advances are made and understanding grows. **The reality of one human race slams the door on the notion of biological "interracial" marriage.**

Some Christians incorrectly apply Acts 17:26 to say different cultural groups shouldn't marry, but this is only about the dispersion of nations and has nothing to do with marriage. Others argue that when 2 Corinthians 6:14 says, "Don't be unequally yoked," it means two people from two different people groups can't marry. However, once one reads the whole verse in context, that argument is paraded as the rubbish it is. Here's the entire verse:

Do not be unequally yoked with unbelievers. For what partnership has righteousness with lawlessness? Or what fellowship has light with darkness?

So yes, we shouldn't be unequally yoked . . . with unbelievers. Applying this concept to marriage means that a Christian is prohibited from knowingly marrying a non-Christian. The biological fact is, there is only one race. **Spiritual fact** — all humans are divided into two races. The difference between the two spiritual races? The direction they're racing. Those in Christ are racing toward the light and those who reject Christ are running headlong into the darkness.

BIBLE REF.
Joshua 2:8–13
Ruth 1:16
Malachi 2:15
Acts 17:26
2 Corinthians 6:14
Ephesians 5:22–33

This verse has absolutely nothing to do with marrying someone with a different skin shade, accent, or birthplace. Applied to marriage, it has everything to do with honoring and glorifying God with the institution He created back in Genesis. **Christians marry someone of the same spiritual race to become one flesh, to produce godly offspring (Malachi 2:15), and to be a picture of Christ and His bride, the Church (Ephesians 5:22–33).**

It's interesting that the prohibition against "interracial" marriage, even in the Old Testament, has always been spiritual. Take for example Rahab the Canaanite and Ruth the Moabite. Both married Israelites and it wasn't a problem. Why did Rahab hide the spies? She knew that the God of Israel was the one true God and had given Jericho into Israel's hands (Joshua 2:8–13). Ruth passionately proclaimed to Naomi before setting out for Israel, "Your people will be my people and your God my God" (Ruth 1:16; NIV). They both believed in the God of Israel; thus, both were of the same spiritual race as the Israelites they married. And by the way, both of those ladies are in the direct lineage of Jesus Christ!

It's worth mentioning that those looking to marry should bear in mind that the notion of **"missionary dating" is nowhere in Scripture.**[1] If a Christian is to marry a Christian, then it only makes sense that they date, or court, only Christians. Also, when marrying someone from a considerably different culture, wisdom, counsel, and prayer should saturate the process. Ultimately, if you're both Christians, then you're both of the same spiritual race with the ultimate eternal commonality in Christ!

---

1 Missionary dating is a religious person who dates another person in order to change that person's beliefs. Consider the negative examples of Solomon in 1 Kings 11:1–4 and Nehemiah 13:26 and Ahab in 1 Kings 16:31.

Doesn't the Bible condone slavery?

The short answer is no. There are at least three keys to understanding this issue biblically — context, context, context.

The word for "slave" in the Bible is also rightly translated as "servant" or "bondservant." In essence, there are two kinds of slavery described in the Bible: a paid servant or bondservant, and harsh enslavement without pay.

The Bible unequivocally condemns harsh slavery. **The brutal "race-based" slavery that plagued the west for centuries is utterly anti-biblical and denounced by God's Word!** Slave traders ("kidnappers/men stealers") are listed among the worst of sinners in 1 Timothy 1:10. Exodus 21:16 declares,

He who kidnaps a man, whether he sells him or he is found in his possession, shall surely be put to death. (NASB)

This sort of biblically decried slavery is what most people think of when they hear the word **slavery. However, an important rule in hermeneutics, rightly interpreting the Bible, is to read the text in context.** Haphazardly attempting to squeeze ideas into the biblical, historical text typically leads to misinterpretation. Such is the case here.

The type of "slavery" described and regulated in the Bible was entirely different from "harsh slavery." Basically, it's a type of bankruptcy law for someone who had lost themselves to debt with no way to repay. It was an economical arrangement of

BIBLE REF.
Exodus 21:16
Leviticus 25:38–46
Ephesians 6:5–9
Colossians 4:1
1 Timothy 1:10

sorts with the goal of eliminating debt. The debtor would go to the person they were indebted to, or another wealthy person, and voluntarily offer themselves as a bond-servant. If the person agreed, **the bondservant had his debt covered, on-the-job training in a particular skill, a place to live, and made a wage. After six years, the bondservant's agreement was fulfilled, their loan fully paid, and they were set free**. A friend of mine joked that it sounds better than college!

There were many regulations regarding this practice and those participating. These protocols, properly understood in context, are clearly given to protect all parties involved. It was also to prevent this form of "bond-servitude" from becoming the cruel, inhumane slavery practiced by surrounding cultures and throughout history (Leviticus 25:38–46; Ephesians 6:5–9, Colossians 4:1). These regulations are yet another repudiation of the detestable act of brutal slavery.

It's worth noting that Christians — like William Wilberforce and Abraham Lincoln — led the charge to abolish the atrocity of harsh, race-based slavery in the west. Christians who stood firm on God's Word understood that all people are made in God's image and refused to compromise with the popular ideology of their day. **Many historians credit Christian thought and action for the abolition of slavery in almost every country.** The countries that still practice slavery today are typically polytheistic or Muslim.

In the secular worldview — with evolution, no god, relative morality, humans equated to earthworms — why not condone or even celebrate ruthless slavery? Especially if it's beneficial for you.

Secularists trying to play "gotcha" with this question are out of luck. **Only Christianity can account for the equality of humanity and the repudiation of vicious slavery.**

Isn't the Bible sexist?

The Bible's first chapter annihilates this fallacious secular claim. Genesis 1:27 says:

God created man in his own image, in the image of God he created him; male and female he created them.

Men and women uniquely and equally display the image of God. Therefore, both have indelible and identical value, dignity, and worth.

The Bible also unapologetically proclaims the diversity of men and women just as authoritatively as it declares their equality. The assigning of different attributes, roles, and positions in no way affects God's appointed human value. The value of a teacher and student, boss and employee, coach and player, man and woman are the same. **This principle is most dynamically displayed in the Trinity. God the Son gladly submits to God the Father in their different roles even though they are equal in essence, power, and glory** (Luke 22:42; John 6:38; 1 Corinthians 15:28).

In creating Adam first, God signified his unique role as leader under the authority of God and for God's glory alone (1 Corinthians 11:3). The responsibility of leadership is to be performed with a servant's heart that models and magnifies the sacrificial love of Christ for the church displayed ultimately on the Cross (Ephesians 5:23–33). Genesis records that God created Eve from Adam with the role of helpmate (or helper). Lest one believe the title of "helper" is insignificant, God is repeatedly referred to as a "helper" to man throughout Scripture (Psalm

BIBLE REF.
Psalm 30:10, 54:4
Luke 22:42
Acts 2:38, 16:14
Romans 3:9–12, 23
1 Corinthians 11:3
Galatians 3:26–29
Ephesians 5:23–33

30:10, 54:4, 118:7; Hebrews 13:6). The responsibility of the position is one of gentle strength where the woman uses her gifts and abilities to support and aid the man in his sacrificial leading (Ephesians 5:23–33).

The distinctive roles and attributes of His image bearers do not vary their worth. **Rather, the creative variety is complementary to each other and exceedingly** glorifying **to the Creator.**

Also, women are esteemed throughout the Bible as their virtuous acts in and outside the home are recorded. Miriam (Exodus 15:20–21), Deborah (Judges 4), Ruth, Esther, noble wife of Proverbs 31, Lydia (Acts 16:14), to name a few. And don't forget that when Jesus rose from the dead He appeared first to the women, a powerful testimony of their worth in His eyes.

The Bible declares the equality of men and women as innate sinners in need of saving (Romans 3:9–12, 23; Psalm 53:1, 143:2). It declares their equality as believers. To be saved, God's requirement for all — males and females alike — is repentance and faith (Acts 2:38; Romans 10:9). Once saved, the status of redeemed, justified, righteous, and adopted is the same for either gender (Galatians 3:26–29).

None of these biblical principles can consistently be applied in the secular worldview. In the absence of God-ordained value and morality, why shouldn't men oppress women as has occurred throughout history? Secularism and evolutionary philosophy have no cogent response, but the Bible does. No, the Bible is not sexist, but one has to ask why isn't the secularist?

What's the biblical take on feminism?

Feminism is often described as happening in three major waves. The first one started in the 1800s and focused on legal inequalities for women, particularly voting rights. The second wave, launched in the 1960s, expanded the movement to address perceived cultural and societal inequalities. It implored women to realize they could find identity outside of childbearing and homemaking. In the 1990s, the third wave began, seeking to further unveil and address the layers of oppression experienced by women globally due to multiple intersecting factors like race, gender, ethnicity, class, religion, etc.

What's feminism in summary? A short version of the basic definition you'll find is the theory of and movement(s) for the equality of the sexes. But this is where the water immediately gets muddy. What do you mean by equality? Who defines it and its implications? Again, either God does, or humans do.

As covered in the last chapter, God established the equality of the sexes by making both in His image (Genesis 1:27) — equal in value, worth, personhood, sinfulness, and salvation. However, they are not the same. **Each gender equally and uniquely displays God's image and glory with different attributes, roles, and functions for His purposes.**

Directly opposing this, feminism today has the apparent goal of defining equality as sameness. Not only are the sexes equal in value and personhood, but also in role and function. All the same options and opportunities for life should be available to

BIBLE REF.

Genesis 1:27
Isaiah 43:11–13
I Corinthians 12:12–18
Galatians 3:28

all because there's no real difference between the genders. Differences in biology are inconsequential.

This is where feminism goes off the rails. Early on it accomplished some good things. Establishing the equality of dignity and value of women within society is good and biblical. Actually, only the Bible can rightly demand these things. Feminism has moved from those things to **redefining womanhood** and indirectly, if not directly, attempting to redefine manhood. This has done tremendous damage to the institution of marriage, the family, biblical gender roles, society, and the church.

Feminism has progressed to the point of opposing all authority, even the Creator's. The root of its rebellion is traced all the way back to Genesis 3 — either submit to God or you become like God.

It's a revolt common to both sexes. Males and females equally struggle to submit to God's design and commands because they're both equally sinful. Males struggle in a different way. There's an epidemic among men who, partially in concession to the feministic ideology, passively or aggressively reject their God-assigned role and task of servant leader. Refusing to surrender to God's commands and yielding to selfish desires, men redefine themselves and their roles into something that's more comfortable, less contentious, and unbiblical. This rebellion has been no less catastrophic than feminism.

Simply put, no one has the right to define themselves. That right is God's alone. And since He made us and loves us beyond understanding, He knows and desires what's best for us. The question for both sexes is will we trust and obey?

Are social justice and intersectionality part of the Gospel?

No. To understand why, they must first be defined.

The modern secular notion of social justice is the quest for equality in terms of distribution of wealth, opportunities, and privileges for individuals within society. As a movement, it seeks to identify the oppressed — those who've been wrongly denied equal access to these things — and to right societal wrongs through empowerment and redistribution — to bring about social justice.

This is where the recent innovation of intersectionality comes in. Not only does it help to identify the oppressed (and oppressors), but levels of oppression and those most in need of reparation and privilege. It's the idea that there are intersecting and compounding layers of oppression due to multiple factors like race, gender, sexuality, ethnicity, class, religion, etc. The more victim categories one belongs to, the heavier their oppression, the more weight their voice carries, and the greater their empowerment within society. For example, a woman's voice has more weight than a man's; if she's African American, she's more empowered; and if she's also lesbian, she has even more authority.

With those definitions understood, **let's hurry to say that many injustices have occurred and are occurring. They're the tragic, temporary consequences of living in a sin-cursed world that will be annihilated when Christ returns. The current world is an unjust place because it's filled with**

BIBLE REF.
Leviticus 19:15
Deuteronomy 15:10–11
Micah 6:8
Romans 3:23–26, 6:23
2 Corinthians 5:21
Philippians 2:7–8
James 1:27, 2:9
Revelation 19:11

unjust sinners. **And of course, God is concerned with justice!** The Bible is replete with commands to act justly with impartiality toward the rich or poor (Micah 6:8; Exodus 23:2–3; Leviticus 19:15; James 2:9) and to care for the needy, the widow, and the orphan (1 John 3:17–18; Deuteronomy 15:10; James 1:27). Christians should be, and typically are, at the forefront, fighting against injustice, partiality, and oppression.

But who defines justice? Answer: God.
He alone defines justice for now and forever.
And justice never has an adjective in the Bible. There aren't variations of justice, simply justice and injustice. Justice exists because there's a just God, who's the source of morality. People recognize injustice because they're made in God's image. Injustice exists because people are sinners. And though some have endured varying egregious hardships, all have violated God's law, and all are accountable to His perfect justice. No exceptions. That's the Christian's primary concern.

Only God is just, and He will judge the unjust (Deuteronomy 32:4; Revelation 19:11). How can we survive His righteous judgment? By repenting of our sin and putting our faith in Christ, the God who left His privilege to purchase our salvation and righteousness (Romans 3:23–25; Philippians 2:7–8; 2 Corinthians 5:21). In this, He is both just and justifier (Romans 3:26).

Social justice and intersectionality are not part of the gospel. They're ambiguous man-centered ideas attempting to classify privileged and oppressed, who's to blame and who's owed. Their basic message is "I'm owed and deserve compensation." The Bible's message is that we all deserve death, but God's free gift is eternal life through Christ who made reparation for all sin (Romans 6:23)!

What about the inequality of genocide?

Attempting to disprove the existence of the biblical God by attacking His morality is quite popular today. The fantastic irony is that without the God of Scripture — the standard and definition of goodness — there is no absolute standard for morality by which to morally judge anyone. From the start, the secularist is caught in a vicious catch-22.

One of the more popular forms of this is to accuse God of injustice by commanding the destruction of so-called innocent peoples. "How could God command Israel to destroy the Canaanites? Or what about killing everyone on earth with a flood? He's an unfair, genocidal bully!"

How does the Christian respond? **First, no one is innocent.** All have sinned, all fall short of God's perfect standard, none seek after God (Matthew 19:17; Romans 3:10–12, 23). Only those who had sinned died (Ezekiel 18:4). **Many people ask, "Why does God let (or cause) bad things to happen to good people?" Well, that only happened once. It was Jesus, who was without sin, who volunteered.**

Not only are none innocent, but the depravity of those destroyed was so obscene that if any sane person could see their acts on the news today, they would likely demand intervention. The Bible records that the wickedness of the pre-Flood people was to the point that all of their thoughts and desires were only evil all the time (Genesis 6:5). The Canaanites that God ordered Israel to eradicate practiced severe brutality, incest, idolatry,

BIBLE REF.
Genesis 6:3, 6:5
Jeremiah 18:7–8
Ezekiel 18:4
Jonah 3
Matthew 19:17
Romans 3:10–12, 23
Romans 1:18–32

homosexuality, bestiality, cultic prostitution, and grotesque child sacrifice. And lest one think God was showing partiality, He warned Israel He would similarly judge them if they emulated the Canaanites.

God's decree against the Canaanites, pre-Flood people, and other similar cases wasn't cruel or vindictive. **Rather, their evil was so oppressive and cancerous that the only option was complete removal. Like a doctor who removes a cancer to save the body, the gangrenous wickedness of those utterly depraved must be removed.** Not to do so would doom Israel and other surrounding nations to suffer a slow death.

There was also plenty of time to repent before judgment fell (Genesis 6:3). The consistent pattern in Scripture is when a nation repents, God withholds judgment (Jeremiah 18:7–8; Jonah 3). Those under the threat of judgment knew what God required and that judgment was coming (2 Peter 2:5). **Yet they willfully refused to save themselves, their families, or other loved ones by submitting to God and repenting of sin.**

Really, arguments like these are just another excuse to suppress the truth (Romans 1:18–32). What the judgments of God in the Bible actually show are God's incredible patience, mercy, love, common grace, sovereignty, righteousness, and holiness. **All of this points to the eternal reality that as a just judge, God will judge all sin without fail.** And just as the Ark was the only means of rescue before the Flood, repentance and faith in Christ is the only means of deliverance from the coming eternal judgment (2 Peter 3:9; 1 Peter 3:18).

Event/people	Were they sinning?	Did God provide justice?	Did God provide a means of salvation?
The Fall: Adam and Eve	Yes	Yes	Yes
The Flood	Yes	Yes	Yes
Sodom and Gomorrah	Yes	Yes	Yes
The Egyptians	Yes	Yes	Yes
The Canaanites	Yes	Yes	Yes
The Benjamites	Yes	Yes	Yes
Non-Christians	Yes	Yes	Yes

LIFE

Marriage, Sexual, & Gender Issues

LOVE is love

What's the origin and definition of marriage?

In order to define marriage properly, one would need a trustworthy, authoritative, historical source. This is why those who swim in the waters of secular humanism and evolutionary thinking are so nebulous about the subject of marriage. In evolutionary thinking, marriage essentially evolved over time in human societies as people perceived it to be more advantageous in civilized living. From this perspective, marriage is not an unchanging divine institution but rather a moldable and disposable social construct.

Christians, however, know better (or at least they should). Why? Because we have a trustworthy, authoritative, eyewitness account from the Creator of marriage Himself! **Marriage finds its genesis in Genesis. In Genesis, marriage's origin, definition, and purpose are revealed per the Creator's will.** In Genesis 2:7–25, the origin of marriage unfolds as God creates the first man and it wasn't good for him to be alone. Then God creates a woman from Adam's rib (an event the Apostle Paul refers to as real history in 1 Corinthians 11:8, 12), bringing to Adam his equal, counterpart, companion, and helper. Adam is so excited he breaks out in poetry, "This at last is bone of my bones and flesh of my flesh!" (Genesis 2:23). In verse 24, the divine institution of marriage is ordained and defined, "Therefore a man shall leave his father and his mother and hold fast to his wife, and they shall become one flesh." And finally, Genesis 1:26–28 and 2:18–25 informs the reader that the purpose of marriage is

BIBLE REF.
Genesis 1:26–28
Genesis 2:7–25, 18–25
Matthew 19:3–5
1 Corinthians 11:8, 12
Ephesians 5:22–33

companionship, completeness, enjoyment, blessing, and fruitfulness, which leads to the multiplying, filling, and subduing decreed by God. The New Testament reveals that marriage has the privilege of being a picture of Christ and His bride, the Church (Ephesians 5:22–33). **As God created man in His image, marriage was created in the image of God's eternal union with His people.**

Marriage is God's idea and God's institution. It's His gift for humanity's good and His glory. In the sacred text of that first biblical book, the origin, definition, and purpose of marriage is discovered. Today's clash over marriage is fundamentally a battle over authority. Either the Bible is acknowledged as God's Word and ultimate authority, or man's ideas are arbitrarily followed.

To effectively deal with today's attack on marriage, Christians must understand the foundational nature of the battle and unflinchingly stand on God's Word to define and defend this biblical institution. And, as we'll see in more detail in a bit, that's exactly what Jesus did (Matthew 19:3–5).

Sex, God's creation & gift

Sex is God's idea. The same God who made galaxies, flowers, humans, marriage, etc., also created sex. He made it, and He defines what it is — its boundaries, proper use, and purpose. This truth is easily missed today because of the world's utter twisting of God's good creation and the silence, compromise, or miseducation of much of the church.

So, starting from the Creator's authoritative Word, how is sex to be understood? It is prescribed and defined in the limited confines of marriage. As summarized in the last chapter, God established marriage and defined it as one man, one woman, for life (Genesis 2:20–25) — a reality repeatedly affirmed by Jesus (Matthew 19; Mark 10). After creating Adam and Eve — and marriage — God blessed them and told them to have lots of children. Genesis 1:28 says:

> *And God blessed them. And God said to them, "Be fruitful and multiply and fill the earth and subdue it . . ."*

Here we see the first family, ordained by God as the foremost human institution for human flourishing. He then declares everything as "very good" (Genesis 1:31).

God's design for sex, then and now (Hebrews 13:4), **is the beautiful, intimate union between a husband and wife** (1 Corinthians 7:3–5). A whole book of the Bible, Song of Solomon, is focused on this very thing! **A union that leads to the creation of "image-bearers," vividly displays the reality of "one-flesh," and is a representation of the eternal intimacy between Christ and His bride, the Church.**

BIBLE REF.
Genesis 2:20–25
Exodus 20:14
Leviticus 18
Matthew 5:27–28, 19
Romans 13:13
1 Corinthians 6:9, 7:3–5
Ephesians 5:3
Hebrews 13:4

However, man's sin corrupted everything. Since that time, mankind has found any number of ways to sinfully distort and abuse God's precious gift of sex. The examples of sexual brokenness that could be listed from today or Scripture are overwhelming. Continually throughout the Bible, God is reminding His people to be holy like He is and to keep sex in its proper God-given place (Exodus 20:14; Leviticus 18; Deuteronomy 22:5, 22; Romans 13:13; 1 Corinthians 6:9; Ephesians 5:3; Colossians 3:5). Jesus even commanded that sexual thoughts are restricted to their proper marriage setting (Matthew 5:27–28). God even cares about marriages becoming non-sexual (1 Corinthians 7:3–5). **Any sexual activity outside of the biblical parameters ordained by God at creation is sinful, broken, and leads to dire, even catastrophic, consequences.**

The old analogy of sex to fire is a good one. A fire in its proper setting, a fireplace, is wonderful, beautiful, and purposeful. A fire outside of its proper place is rapidly and ferociously destructive. This is the reality of sex. Since sex is God's creation, He knows how it works best. And since God's love for humanity can't be fathomed, we can trust that His boundaries for His creation and for His image bearers are good and for our best. If we do fall into sexual sin, the greatest news is that the author of sex is also the author of salvation. All sins, including sexual ones, were paid for at the Cross for those who repent and put their faith in Christ!

The abandonment of God's design for sex

No doubt the cultural "norm" for sexual activity today is a radical departure from the dominant view of generations past. Because of man's sinful nature, there has been sexual revolt throughout history. The difference today is that what started as cultural seeds of rebellion against a generally biblical view of sex have progressively blossomed and rapidly spread to become the "new normal" for sex today.

What dam broke that unleashed the torrent of this new sexual morality? Biblical authority. **The current sexual revolution is a reflection of our culture's utter abandonment of Scripture.** A progressive attack on the credibility of God's Word, particularly its history, has been chipping away at biblical authority for multiple generations.

In a real sense, when Christians gave up the Bible's authority in regard to history, we detached the Bible from the real world. In essence, Christians were saying that the Bible's right about spiritual things but not really connected to the actual world. Initially, this disconnect was applied to origins, but then progressive generations disconnected the Bible from morality. **If the Bible gets something as basic as origins wrong, why trust it with something as "complex" as contemporary morality and sexuality?** This has led to multiple generations — inside and outside the church — who don't truly believe the Bible's authoritative teaching on history, morality, or sexuality. Thus, it has no tangible bearing on everyday life.

BIBLE REF.
Jeremiah 17:9
Proverbs 14:12
Hebrews 13:4
1 Corinthians 6:18

With this in mind, it's fairly easy to see why so many today, even inside the church, no longer have a biblical worldview on issues like origins, marriage, abortion, and sex. The bottom line is, once you give up the absolute authority of God's Word, man's ideas are all you're left with.

If man determines truth, then which man? Today's answer: all of them! Without an absolute, objective standard, each person decides their own truth for all things, including sex. How? Well, **without a divine revelation outside of ourselves, we're ultimately guided by our thoughts, feelings, and appetites.** Sure, people will listen to the ideas of others through conversations, books, and media. And eventually it will be the individual who will judge all that's heard and deliver the verdict. That person has now become his own god.

Our present enlightened mantra is "Follow your heart and do what makes you happy!"

This is how "free sex" became "normal." Each person is encouraged to follow "their heart" and pursue sexual fulfillment however they see fit. But the cataclysmic error with this thinking is plain within Scripture: the heart of man is deceitful, wicked, and sick (Jeremiah 17:9). There is a way that seems right to a man, but it ends in destruction (Proverbs 14:12). This destruction is seen most vividly in the dramatic increase in premarital sex, pornography, abortion, divorce, sex trafficking, and prostitution since the embracing of secular sexuality.

The abandoning of biblical authority left man holding the reins of his sexuality. The

result? The current confusion of sexuality and the many destroyed lives in the wake of the Enemy's lies.

How should Christians respond to homosexuality, gay "marriage," and the "gay Christian"?

In truth and love (Ephesians 4:15). These two things are inextricably linked. As Christians, we've been commanded to do both and should do so joyously out of love for God and His image bearers (1 Corinthians 13; Ephesians 4:15).

The unmistakable truth articulated throughout Scripture is that homosexuality is sin (Leviticus 18:22; Romans 1:26–32; 1 Timothy 1:10; 1 Corinthians 6:9–11). It's a result of the Fall and mankind's sinful nature, in direct rebellion to God's commands and created order (Genesis 1:27–28; Malachi 2:15; Mark 10:6–9; 1 Corinthians 7:2–3).

Biblically speaking, there is no such thing as gay "marriage." As stated earlier, marriage is God's creation, and He alone defines it. He emphatically does so throughout His revealed Word as **a lifelong union between one man and one woman. Anything other than that, no matter what people call it, is** not marriage. It's another thing.

And what about the so called "gay Christian"? Again, it doesn't exist biblically. When someone experiences salvation by submitting and following Christ, they become a Christian. Period. Praise God, their identity is fully found in Christ alone (Galatians 2:20, 3:26–29)! **There's never a descriptor attached to Christian. And a Christian is certainly never identified by their sin, past or present.** You don't see the "promiscuous Christian," "lying Christian," "kleptomaniacal Christian," "raping Christian," or the "violent Christian." As ludicrous as

BIBLE REF.
Leviticus 18:22
Malachi 2:15
Mark 10:6–9
Romans 1:28–32
1 Corinthians 6:9–11
Galatians 2:20, 3:26–29
Ephesians 4:15, 25–32
1 Timothy 1:10

those sound, that's what the title "gay Christian" is doing. **It's attaching a rebellious sin to the identity purchased by Christ who paid for and removed that very sin.**

The basic idea behind the argument for the gay Christian is that some people are born with a homosexual orientation. They're just "born that way." The orientation isn't necessarily bad, it just shouldn't be acted on or only in a monogamous way. The problems with this are myriad. For starters, there is currently no biological or genetic basis for homosexuality. None. In theory, it's plausible that one could be found in the future. What would that prove? It would simply affirm the biblical truth that sin broke everything. It corrupted the entire universe, including humans, from our DNA to the way we think, feel, and perceive reality.

Ultimately, humans have sinful inclinations of all different sorts because we're all sinners. And having a sinful inclination, orientation, or desire does not justify the desire and certainly does not make it good, right, or normative. Someone inclined to violence is not justified in beating his wife. Someone oriented toward promiscuity isn't justified in adultery. An attraction to children does not validate pedophilia. Whatever the surrounding factors influencing a sin, it's still sin. And if you're a follower of Christ, that sin has been paid for on the Cross and you can rejoice in your identity as a Christian!

As we speak these truths, our motivation is love. Love for God, love for His Word, and love for sinners who need a Savior (2 Timothy 2:24–25).

Why do Christians harp on homosexuality when Jesus never mentioned it?

Jesus did address it — numerous times in fact. For instance, in Matthew 5 and 19, Jesus addresses the issue of marriage. While doing so, He does something "radical" that many Christians are unwilling to do today. He quoted the Bible as the authority! **He defines marriage by quoting Genesis 1:27 and 2:24, rooting His understanding of marriage in the history and biology of Genesis.** Here, marriage is defined as one man and one woman for the purposes of procreation, sanctification, and illustration. He states that what God has joined in marriage, let no man separate (Matthew 19:6). The point? God established and defines marriage, not man. Marriage is God's **institution** and man has no right or authority to redefine it in any way. By definition, same-sex "marriage" is not marriage. It's an arbitrary man-made concept that goes directly against what God created in Genesis and what Jesus unreservedly affirmed and proclaimed.

Some suggest that Jesus' lack of stating the word homosexuality during His earthly ministry implies acceptance. However, that's illogical and leads to huge problems. For example, Jesus never mentioned pedophilia by name either. Does He accept that? Of course not!

More significantly, Jesus is God. He is a member of the Trinity, the singular being of God existing eternally in three persons — the Father, Son, and Holy Spirit. As such, **Jesus is the ultimate author of all Scripture,** not just the "red letters." He's the author of Leviticus 18 and Romans 1.

BIBLE REF.
Genesis 1:27, 2:24
Leviticus 18
Matthew 5, 19, 19:6
John 3
Romans 1
2 Timothy 3:16
Revelation 22:15

Jesus was there, executing righteous judgment on Sodom and Gomorrah. All of Scripture is "God-breathed" (2 Timothy 3:16; NIV). When any Scripture speaks, Jesus speaks. And there are hundreds of Bible verses that deal directly with sexuality, marriage, and sexual purity.

It must also be stated that the Bible is one book. It's one book, composed of smaller books, with one fundamental author, God. These books are supernaturally unified in truth, theme, and focus and cannot be divided one from the other. **Every verse of Scripture is eventually to be understood in the grand context of the Bible's singular meta-narrative.** That narrative, from one end of the Bible to the other, points to Jesus Christ. In reality, all of history is "His-story"! It's often said like this: the best commentary on the Bible is the Bible. This makes sense because it's the absolute authority. **Understanding this means Leviticus 18 cannot be separated or isolated from John 3.** The teaching of Christ cannot be separated from the Apostles' teaching. The Apostles were Christ's Apostles; their teaching is the authoritative teaching of the church from King Jesus.

As God, Jesus dealt with homosexuality directly and indirectly. In His perfect, indivisible Word, homosexuality is plainly addressed in the larger, unified context of revealing the one who can save us from our sins and the final judgment (Revelation 22:15).

CHAPTER 19

Divorce Mk 10:1-16; Lk 18:15-17

nd it came to pass, ^R*that* when Jesus had finished these sayings, he departed from Galilee, and came into the ^Tcoasts of Ju-dae'-a beyond Jordan;

Mk 10:1-12 • *region*

2 ^RAnd great multitudes followed him; and he healed them there.

Ma 12:15

3 The Pharisees also came unto him, ^Ttempting him, and saying unto him, Is it lawful for a man to ^Tput away his wife for ^Tevery cause?

testing • divorce • any reason

4 And he answered and said unto them, Have ye not read, that he which made *them* at the beginning ^Rmade them male and fe-male,

Ge 1:27; 5:2

5 And said, ^RFor this cause shall a man leave father and mother, and shall cleave to his wife: and they twain shall be one flesh?

Ge 2:24

6 Wherefore they are ^Tno more twain, but e flesh. What therefore God hath joined her, let not man put asunder. *no longer two*

It's all about love!
Love wins!

"Love wins!" is the popular rallying cry of the LGBTQ+ movement. It's often used to shut down Christian opposition or to justify Christian inclusion. The argument is typically, "The Bible's all about love, God is love, Christians should be all about love, so how can you be against people loving each other? Love is love!" It's been so effective because who wants to argue against love?

However, who defines what love is? Once again, the choices are God or man. A man's attempt to define love is eventually arbitrary because someone else can just as easily define it differently. And if everything is solely the result of natural processes, then "love" is nothing more than a chemical reaction in the brain no different in essence to the chemical reaction of "hate."

God, the author of humanity, marriage, knowledge, natural laws, beauty, and all of reality, is the author and definer of love as well. **Fundamentally, love is an action, accompanied by emotion, done for the benefit of another** (John 3:16, 15:12–13; Romans 5:8; 1 John 3:16). Love necessarily requires relationship, which is why only the biblical worldview can reliably explain it. **The perfect relationship of the three Persons within the triune Godhead is the source of the intangible reality of love and a unique experience of humans as God's image bearers.** No other worldview — whether originally there was nothing, a force, a singular god, or multiple disconnected gods — can consistently explain the existence of genuine love.

BIBLE REF.
Deuteronomy 6:5, 7:9
Matthew 22:37–40
John 3:16, 15:12–13
Romans 5:8, 13:8–14
1 Corinthians 13
1 John 3:16, 5:3
2 John 1:6

PRIDE

LOVE IS LOVE

The love that originates and emanates from the biblical God is rooted in His nature and truth. **Anything not in line with His nature and truth isn't love, it's actually antagonistic toward authentic love.** Thus, the connection between God's love and His law are the constant correlation of love to obedience (1 John 5:3; 2 John 1:6; Deuteronomy 6:5, 7:9).

In Matthew 22:37–40, Jesus was asked by the Pharisees what the greatest commandment is. He basically responded that all the Old Testament commands are summarized with love God with all you've got and love others like you love yourself. In Romans 13:8–14, we again are told to love one another, and love does no wrong to a neighbor. What things are wrong? The things against God's law, the Ten Commandments, God's Word. Love for God and others is inextricably linked to obedience to God's law, the standard for truth.

Now to 1 Corinthians 13, the renowned "Love Chapter" that illuminates the prominence and qualities of love. Verse 6 reveals a powerful truth for today: "It (love) does not rejoice at wrongdoing but rejoices with the truth." **Love, biblically and rightly understood, can never encompass homosexuality. Why? Because by definition, homosexuality is wrongdoing and love doesn't rejoice in wrongdoing.** By definition, homosexuality is not love.

God's love cannot be separated from God's truth. The greatest truth is that sin and death have been conquered by the love of Christ. Perfect love has already won. Love won at the Cross!

Why do Christians "pick and choose" from Leviticus?

Leviticus 18:22 is an often-cited verse that condemns homosexuality. Yet critics of the Bible eagerly point out there are numerous rules listed in Leviticus that Christians don't follow today. The question then follows, "Why do you pick and choose? Why do you choose to apply Levitical laws on homo-sexuality but disregard Levitical laws against wearing clothes of blended fabrics and eating pork or shrimp?"

At its root, this question is the accusation that the Christian is being a hypocrite. Response?

Start by pointing out that the critic is borrowing biblical principles, which he rejects, to argue against the Bible. Only Christianity, with absolute truth and morality from an absolute God, can rightly say hypocrisy is wrong. Declaring all truth as relative, the secularist has no coherent reason to label hypocrisy as bad.

Next, **everyone picks and chooses.** But by what standard? Ironically, the secularist even picks and chooses from Leviticus. Leviticus also condemns slander, lying, stealing, and perverting justice (Leviticus 19). Why does the critic agree those things are wrong while rejecting other parts of Leviticus that denounce homosexuality? He's arbitrarily picking what suits his palate with himself as the decisive authority.

The Christian picks and chooses in light of all of God's Word. As mentioned earlier, the Bible is one book with one meta-narrative. Every biblical verse and principle are to be

BIBLE REF.
Leviticus 18:22, 19
Matthew 15:11
Mark 10:6–9
Romans 1:20, 26–27
1 Corinthians 6:9–11
Colossians 1:15–20
1 Timothy 1:9–10, 4:4

understood in the larger context of the entirety of the Bible. God's self-revelation of His unchanging divine nature and attributes culminating in Christ is the overarching theme of Scripture (Romans 1:20; Colossians 1:15–20). Every biblical precept, teaching, and law reflect this unwavering foundation while pointing to Jesus.

As history and revelation unfold in time, God's will, nature, and intended order for creation are eternally steadfast. Their expression in given laws and penalties, to different peoples at different times, has varied while still rooted in the same unchanging principles. In the old covenant, certain civil laws were given to Israel in the ancient near east for them to operate as a culture then and there and to separate them from the surrounding pagan cultures. Some of those laws cannot be rationally applied to our culture today, just as many of our laws would be nonsensical to them. Ancient Israel was also given unique ceremonial laws that guided their worship. Their definitive purpose was to point to Christ, in whom they found their ultimate fulfillment in the new covenant.

Homosexuality's violation of God's will and created order is condemned in both the old and new covenants. Jesus, like Genesis, defined marriage as a man and a woman (Mark 10:6–9). Paul, like Leviticus, denounces homosexuality (Romans 1:26–27; 1 Timothy 1:9–10) and rejoices with believers set free from that sin (1 Corinthians 6:9–11). In contrast, the old food restrictions aren't applied in the new covenant. Jesus and Paul make this clear (Matthew 15:11; 1 Timothy 4:4).

The Christian justifiably, not hypocritically, picks and chooses based on Scripture's total revelation, which consistently displays God's nature and purpose.

How do we respond to the transgender revolution?

The transgender movement has taken the western world by storm. Headlines: changing school regulations allowing transgender children to use whichever bathroom/locker rooms, to play on girls or boys sports teams, a transgender 5-year-old, and a former superstar male athlete being awarded "Woman of the Year" by a popular magazine.[1]

The "transgender" ideology is the basic belief that our "gender identity" is a fluid, changeable social construct that's not confined to our biology. One's "gender identity" is a state of mind and may not match their body, so a "woman" may be trapped in a male body. In such cases, reconstructive "reassignment" surgery is seen as a valid, even necessary, option.

In the last half century our culture has experienced a progressively expanding attack on God's design for humanity and society. The sexual revolution redefined sex, feminism redefined manhood and womanhood, and the homosexual movement redefined sexuality and marriage. Now the transgender revolution seeks to redefine bodily gender realities with seemingly unprecedented velocity.

BIBLE REF.
Isaiah 45:18
Romans 1
1 Corinthians 6:19
1 Corinthians 14:33
2 Peter 1:3

---

1 washingtonpost.com/local/public-safety/battle-over-transgender-student-rights-moves-to-high-school-locker-rooms/2018/04/25/b319365a-3f29-11e8-974f-aacd97698cef_story.html?noredirect=on&utm_term=.ebcff558159f
abcnews.go.com/US/transgender-teens-outrun-track-field-competitors-critics-close/story?id=55856294
nbcnews.com/storyline/transgender-kids/jacob-s-journey-life-transgender-5-year-old-n345131
usmagazine.com/celebrity-news/news/caitlyn-jenner-named-one-of-glamours-women-of-the-year-20152910/
Today's feminism often conflicts with the claims and goals of gender revolutionaries. If the gender revolutionaries are right, anyone can be a female. And whose rights are the feminists fighting for? This has caused conflict amongst liberal ideologues.

The realities of God's created order are being progressively cast aside as we buy the Enemy's lie that true happiness is found in total autonomy. Maximum happiness is discovered by following your own path for truth, sexuality, and gender identity. These things are not fixed God-given gifts, they're a blank canvas for you to paint your own reality for your supreme pleasure. Transgenderism is the newest and grandest expansion into self-rule and rebellion.

As God's wisdom and design are rejected and reviled, confusion concerning sexuality, masculinity, femininity, and gender reign supreme. This has resulted in catastrophic individual and societal consequences that are obvious to the honest observer. However, the biblical God isn't a God of confusion and His Word is sufficient (1 Corinthians 14:33; 2 Peter 1:3). As previously discussed, **sex, sexuality, gender roles, and genders are God's creation and part of His created order. They're good gifts from the Creator given for human flourishing.** Our Maker defines us and tells us our bodies were created for our joy and as a temple of the Holy Spirit (1 Corinthians 6:19). **Our gender was lovingly and intentionally assigned to us by the Creator for our good and His glory.**

The Bible also explains the confusion of individuals and culture: sin. **Man's fall into sin broke creation, humanity, and how we see ourselves. We need God's Word and Spirit to restore what's broken.** Transgenderism is just the newest tenet of our culture's false gospel. Salvation and fulfillment are not found in autonomy but in complete submission to our sovereign Maker and Redeemer.

ALL GENDER TOILETS

LIFE

Environmental Issues

You believe in climate change, don't you?

Yes, climates change. But what causes the fluctuations and what do they mean? Once again, how one answers these questions is entirely dependent on their worldview. And wrong assumptions about the past will lead to wrong conclusions about the present and future.

Secularists wrongly assume that the earth is billions of years old, that the ice sheets of Greenland and Antarctica and tree ring dating accurately "record" climate data for tens of thousands of years, and that the earth's climate has been extremely stable for roughly ten thousand years. Therefore, the minor temperature changes observed today are considered dynamic, extraordinarily rapid, and catastrophic if the trend continues. And trends are expected to continue in a prolonged fashion because that's what they've done for "millions of years." Since these changes occurred in the narrow window of man's technological boom, he's likely to blame. **But this understanding of earth's history is built on one unprovable, anti-biblical assumption after another.** Fundamentally, this model rejects biblical history, the account of earth's history given by the Creator Himself.

God's Word gives the real historical account. The earth is around 6,000 years old, and the original creation and climate were perfect (Genesis 1:31). In Genesis 3, man's sin corrupted all of creation, including the climate (Romans 8:22). Man did cause climate change! Nearly 4,300 years ago, Noah's Flood wrecked and rearranged the earth and its climate (Genesis 6:13).

Post-Flood, there was a transitioning climate, including an ice age that covered about 30% of the earth's land surface in ice. As the world settled and the ice age receded, the transitional climate oscillated and stabilized into the present climate.

Understanding this, **the biblical model expects variations in temperature and powerfully explains actual climate data.** It explains the major temperature/climate changes of centuries ago, long before man-made greenhouse gases. The Medieval Warm Period (A.D. 800–1200) saw average temperatures higher than the warmest years of the past few decades. The Little Ice Age (A.D. 1400–1880) had average cooler temperatures than those of modern times. Apparently, the global temperature cycles around an average temperature that's been slightly warmer in the past. Not appealing to man-made CO_2 for temperature fluctuations makes sense of these often-avoided facts: CO_2 is essential to life (especially plants) and is a good thing, water vapor is responsible for 80–90% of the total greenhouse effect, and man-made CO_2 is responsible for less than 1% of the greenhouse effect.[1]

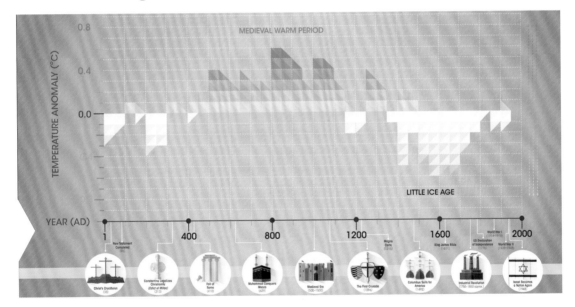

Climate change is the end times apocalypse for secularists. For some, their passion is genuine, and for others, it's seemingly based in a selfish ambition. **But Scripture is explicit that** climate change won't end this world. **The world and its climate will endure until Christ returns** (Genesis 8:22). Then the heavens and earth will be replaced by a new heaven and a new earth (2 Peter 3:7–13; Revelation 21:1–8). This is the "climate change" everyone needs to believe in!

1 https://answersingenesis.org/environmental-science/climate-change/should-we-be-concerned-about-climate-change/

What's a Christian response to the "green movement"?

The green movement has garnered much attention and fanfare. The secular mantras range from leaving the world a better place to honoring/worshiping "Mother Earth" to quarantining the plague and parasite that is humanity.

First, there's only one God, and "Mother Earth/Nature" isn't it. Often in the green movement, nature is deified in various ways, all of which are idolatry. **Nature is not god nor is it worthy of worship.** The biblical God is the one true God, and it's sinful rebellion to worship the creation over the Creator (Romans 1:25). God alone is to be worshiped; as the author of life, nature, and humanity, all are accountable to His decrees for His creation.

Next, humanity isn't a plague or parasite as some melodramatically or seriously suggest. This thinking is consistent, however, within the secular worldview. Humans are accidental chemical reactions that evolved and multiplied to the point of dominating, depleting, and eventually destroying the planet that gave and sustained human life. If humanity's a plague, quarantining the pestilence makes sense. **But if we're just a virus and there's nothing more to reality than our limited random physical existence, why care about future generations or the well-being of the planet? To say something "ought" to be done is to suggest there's an absolute standard for right and wrong that should be adhered to. However, without God, no such higher standard can exist.**

BIBLE REF.
Deuteronomy 25:4
Psalm 104:10–14
Proverbs 6:6–9, 12:10
Isaiah 45:12, 18
Jonah 4:11
Romans 1:25
1 Corinthians 4:2
Luke 12:6–7, 13:6–9

The truth of reality articulated in God's Word couldn't be more different. The earth, made by an all-wise Creator, was meant to be inhabited, particularly by humans, for humanity's good and God's glory. (Isaiah 45:12, 18). **Humanity is no invading virus; humans are the crowning jewel of God's creation** with the amazing privilege and responsibility of bearing God's image!

God commands His image bearers to "fill the earth and subdue it and have dominion" (Genesis 1:28). There's no connotation of tyrannical subjugation or exploitation in these commands. Quite the opposite. **Man is to be a thankful, faithful steward of God's gift of creation. Part of reflecting God's image is wisely using natural resources and kindly managing the animals, plants, and land so that creation blossoms, humanity flourishes, and God is glorified** (Genesis 2:15; Deuteronomy 25:4; Proverbs 6:6–9, 12:10, 27:23–27; Luke 13:6–9). When man rightly obeys and practices loving stewardship, creation and humanity prosper. When man rebels against his Creator's command, wantonly abusing and exploiting creation for selfish gain, both man and creation suffer.

God cares about His creation and we should as well out of love and obedience (Psalm 36:6, 104:10–14, 147:9; Jonah 4:11; Luke 12:6–7, 24). Let us be found faithful stewards of the earth God has entrusted to us (Psalm 24:1; 1 Corinthians 4:2). Our just concern for God's creation should be infinitesimal to our concern, compassion, and care for God's image bearers who will live on for eternity in one of two places long after this world has perished.

What about animal rights?

Who hasn't been moved by those commercials with emotional music, dramatically showing an abused dog? Concern for animals is good and biblical.

However, as our culture frantically runs away from biblical values, its morality is being turned upside down. A growing demand for equality, or supremacy, of animal rights to human rights is a powerful illustration.

As society seeks to expand the legality of murdering humans in the womb or close to the tomb, regulations and legislation protecting animals of all sorts, even unborn, are flooding the law books. Due to the multigenerational influence of evolution and humanism, increasingly the dominant cultural view of animal rights reflects that of PETA (People for the Ethical Treatment of Animals), "When it comes to pain, love, joy, loneliness, and fear, a rat is a pig is a dog is a boy."[1] Basically, "Animals are people too!" Or, people are animals. PETA ran a campaign themed "Holocaust on Your Plate," which equated the barbecuing of chickens to the burning of Jews in the Holocaust.[2]

The inconsistencies of evolutionary thinking in equating animals to people and simultaneously demanding "rights" and a "binding morality" are staggering. If all life evolved and is equal, shouldn't animal rights groups be against killing tapeworms, lice, and even plants? **If humans are just animals, shouldn't they be allowed to steal, kill, commit incest, or be**

BIBLE REF.
Genesis 1:26
Psalm 147:9
Proverbs 27:23–27
Jonah 4:11
Luke 12:22–31

1 "Why Animal Rights?," PETA, http://www.peta.org/about-peta/why-peta/why-animal-rights/
2 http://www.cnn.com/2003/US/Northeast/02/28/peta.holocaust/

a cannibal? Animals do all these things. If animal rights activists were consistent, they shouldn't be upset when a human kills an animal, or human, because it's just one animal killing another.

Most animal rights groups are silent about, or support, the murdering of children in the womb. But if people are animals, shouldn't they care about these babies? They're certainly worried about unborn bald eagles and sea turtles. You can get jail time for simply "disturbing" their eggs.[3] **Ironically, with the rise of humanism, the value of humanity has reached an all-time low in the west.**

In the evolutionary worldview, where do rights come from? **Rights only make sense in the biblical worldview. They're an abstract concept that assumes the unremovable value of something applied by an undeniable absolute authority.** The secularist arguing for rights borrows from Christianity. And if animals are our equal, why don't they argue for animal rights?

As detailed previously, mankind uniquely bears the image of the Creator who gave humanity the task of taking dominion over creation, including the animals (Genesis 1:26). This is not a license for cruelty, oppression, or carelessness. **It's a responsibility of stewardship to be carried out obediently, lovingly, and faithfully —** done for creation's benefit, mankind's flourishing, and the Creator's exaltation.

Although animals are to be cherished and cared for, they're not human nor equal in rights.
Humanity is sacred.
And God's image bearers are profoundly, infinitely, and eternally more important! So important that God Himself became a man to provide a bridge of salvation for humanity.

---

3 https://www.fws.gov/midwest/eagle/protect/laws.html, https://conserveturtles.org/barrier-island-center-sea-turtle-nesting-season/

Are aliens the answer?

Surveys show half of Americans believe intelligent aliens exist.[1] No doubt, a major reason is the dogmatic assertion of many scientists that aliens must exist.

Yet why are the secularists so passionately convinced of aliens? For several reasons, complexity of life being one. Numerous evolutionists argue that a few billion years isn't enough time for life to evolve. Possibly it started evolving somewhere else in the older universe and was later "seeded" on earth by aliens. Maybe aliens even created life! Richard Dawkins, evolutionary biologist and atheist evangelist, thinks it's possible. In an interview for the documentary *Expelled*, he suggested aliens could've evolved, developed sophisticated technology, and "designed a form of life that they seeded onto, perhaps, this planet . . . it's possible that you might find evidence for that if you look at the details of our chemistry, molecular biology, you might find a signature of some sort of designer."[2] **His willing acceptance of aliens as creator but not God is testament to his heart's suppression of truth** (Romans 1:18–23).

1 https://www.newsweek.com/most-people-believe-intelligent-aliens-exist-377965
2 Ben Stein: "What do you think is the possibility that intelligent design might turn out to be the answer to some issues in genetics, or in evolution?" Richard Dawkins: "Well, it could come about in the following way: it could be that at some earlier time, somewhere in the universe, a civilization evolved by probably some kind of Darwinian means to a very, very high level of technology, and designed a form of life that they seeded onto, perhaps, this planet. Now that is a possibility, and an intriguing possibility. And I suppose it's possible that you might find evidence for that if you look at the details of our chemistry, molecular biology, you might find a signature of some sort of designer, and that designer could well be a higher intelligence from elsewhere in the universe. But that higher intelligence would itself have had to have come about by some explicable, or ultimately explicable, process. It couldn't have just jumped into existence spontaneously. That's the point." *Expelled: No Intelligence Allowed* (2008-04-18)

BIBLE REF.
Genesis 1:1–28
Isaiah 45:18
Romans 1:18–23; 8:22
Hebrews 9:27–28, 10:10
1 Peter 3:18

Aliens seem obvious to evolutionists because life isn't a special creation. If it randomly, accidentally happened on earth, surely in this vast universe it happened somewhere else. This reflects the secular notion that the earth isn't special.

But alien life doesn't line up with Scripture. **The earth was uniquely created by God to be inhabited (Isaiah 45:18). Throughout the days of creation, God made various living things and described how they're to live on earth. God made man, His image bearer and crowning glory, to live on earth and have dominion.** Nothing like this is said about any of the other "lights in the expanse" (Genesis 1:14–15). Their purpose and design were different and evidently not intended for life.

The possibility of *intelligent* alien life is more problematic. The Bible says the entire universe was corrupted by sin and the curse (Romans 8:22). If intelligent aliens existed, they would be cursed yet unredeemable. **How can a "Wookiee" or "Vulcan" be saved? They're not blood relatives of Jesus, so His blood doesn't pay their sin debt.** Scripture says Christ died once for all and that Jesus is both God and man, nothing else (1 Peter 3:18; Hebrews 9:27–28, 10:10). God's redemption plan is only for human beings.

Despite all the hype, effort, resources, and money spent, no alien life or signal has been found. Yet secular faith won't die. Why? Along with believing they'd provide powerful proof for evolution, aliens are often presented as beings who'll unravel the universe's mysteries, unveil life's meaning, cure our diseases, fix the world's problems, and usher in utopia. Sound familiar?

They're a "God replacement" that's awfully appealing. You get all the "divine benefits" without accountability and judgment. However, God is irreplaceable and biblical reality is reality. The earth is unique and the spiritual focal point of creation. It's where God visited, became our blood relative, died on a Cross, and defeated death to make a way of salvation for His unique image bearers alone. Sorry, Chewbacca.

Conclusion

Why are you judging when Jesus said judge not?

Most quoted Bible verse today? Probably Matthew 7:1, "Judge not." Also, possibly the most abused verse, usually pried, kicking and screaming, out of context.

It's used to shut down Christians who'd dare make a biblical argument against a popular cultural sin. Say a public word against abortion, fornication, homosexuality, transgenderism, etc., and expect to be bludgeoned with "judge not" and told to be quiet. Better yet, quit being so judgmental and agree with secular judgments.

Problems with secular argumentation on this are legion. **If it's wrong to judge in the secular worldview, then stop judging Christians!** And why would judging be wrong? Without God and absolute standards, no word or action — no matter how judgmental — could rationally be classified as right or wrong. It's all preference, and who are you to judge someone else's preference? **The secularist is trying to use the authority of the Bible they reject to hypocritically judge an action they have no reason to condemn.**

The bottom line is, everyone makes judgments all the time. It's impossible not to because "neutrality" doesn't exist. The real question about judging is by what authority and standard does one judge? The options are twofold — one's authority is either God's Word or their own. And with no absolute authority, secularists hypocritically and arbitrarily judge Christians and offences they dislike, while conveniently judging any judgment against themselves.

BIBLE REF.
Matthew 7
John 7:24
Psalm 7:11, 9:8
Isaiah 33:22
John 5:22
Acts 4:12; 17:31
2 Timothy 2:24–25

The Bible is jammed with commands to judge and to do so rightly. Ironically, this is Jesus' teaching in Matthew 7 when you read the whole passage in context. The critic wants to quote verse 1 for their advantage, while ignoring the rest of the chapter. Jesus commands His followers to make judgments on whom to engage (v. 6), the narrow and the wide gates (v. 13–14), true and false prophets (v. 15–20), true and false disciples (v. 21–23), and "wise and foolish builders" (v. 24–29). Jesus wasn't saying not to judge; He was teaching how to judge!

In verse 5 He says, "You hypocrite, first take the plank out of your own eye, and then you will see clearly to remove the speck from your brother's eye" (NIV). The believer is being warned against making superficial, hypocritical, condemning, self-righteous, "pharisaical" judgments (John 7:24). You judge yourself before making judgments about others by the same standard. What standard? The unmovable rock of Christ's Word described in Matthew 7:24–27. **We're to make right judgments about ourselves and others in light of God's Word, out of love for God and love for people.**

"Only God can judge me." That's right, He will, and that should scare you! God is the perfect, righteous, holy, eternal, supreme Judge of all (Psalm 7:11, 9:8; Isaiah 33:22; John 5:22; Acts 17:31). And the Judge of the universe has made a judgment about salvation — it's through Christ alone (Acts 4:12). That's why Christians are to judge rightly by God's Word, lovingly identifying sin to point people to Christ who alone can save them from the final judgment (2 Timothy 2:24–25).

Don't you want progress and to be on the right side of history?

Yes and yes. Christians want actual biblical progress that leads to real human flourishing and is eternally on the right side of history.

When these arguments are made, the allegation is that Christianity is hindering mankind and that future generations will look back at those who impeded the secular utopia with disdain. **But who determines genuine progress, and which side of history is the right one?** When nonbelievers claim Christianity defies these things, they're drawing a blatant distinction between words and actions they consider right and others they consider to be wrong. However, by what authentic standard are secularists judging (thought you couldn't do that) one person's version of progress as good and another's as bad? Why shouldn't Stalin, Mao, Osama bin Laden, Pol Pot, or Hitler define good progress? As seen repeatedly, the authority of secularists — when traced to the source — is their own arbitrary opinion that they intolerantly and bigotedly force on others without care of offense.

Why should secularists care about progress or coming generations anyway? In their worldview, humanity is a chemical accident, morality is fluid, truth is relative, autonomy is king, and eventually everyone will be extinct with no memory of history preserved. To care for humanity's plight is to again borrow from the Christian worldview.

The biblical worldview is overflowing with earnest reasons to

BIBLE REF.
Job 38–42
Matthew 7:11–14
Matthew 16:26–27
Matthew 22:37–39
Matthew 25:31–46
2 Corinthians 5:10
Philippians 2:9–11

care for humanity. Christians care because all humans are created in God's image and have souls that will eternally exist in either heaven or hell. Christians care because our Creator cares. When Jesus was asked to identify the greatest commandment, He responded by basically saying love God with everything you've got and love people the way you love yourself (Matthew 22:37–39). God cares about the well-being of people and commands His followers to do likewise. Christians care out of love and obedience to God and a desire to imitate and glorify their Creator and Savior.

Yes, Christians want genuine progress for human flourishing. **And there is a book, a "manual," the Word of God, where the** Designer and Maker **of humanity explicitly details how His creation works best.** God's instructions for morality, family, society, marriage, sexuality, gender, stewardship, and dominion are His blueprints for humanity's thriving and fulfillment in His creation.

You want real progress? Follow the directions of the Author, Maker, and Sustainer of the universe. The societies that have done so, directly or indirectly, have been the most civilized, structured, and prosperous in history. Reject God's instructions and the result is regression increasing exponentially over time. This too has played out numerous times in history and is currently happening throughout the west. **Each dysfunction happening today can be traced to some deviation of God's will, plan, and design.**

Reject God's Word, and the only progress you'll make is toward earthly and eventually eternal destruction. Only God's design works in the real world, and there's only one, eternal, right side of history — God's.

Every good thing secularists argue for comes from the Bible

As seen repeatedly, secular arguments are simply opinions without authority. The secular worldview hypocritically demands a specific response that's intolerant of others and out of step with its own professed principles. Since their worldview cannot account for the standard they're claiming, secularists constantly borrow from the biblical worldview to argue against the Bible. Ironically, their ability to argue at all shows they're wrong.

Exposing secularism's inconsistencies, hypocrisy, and arbitrary nature is a potent refutation of that worldview. On the other end of the spectrum, pointing out where we agree with the secularist is equally powerful. Agree with the secularists!? Absolutely! **When you drill down past the emotionalism, logical fallacies, and bad argumentation, at the core of his argument the nonbeliever is typically appealing to some biblical principle we wholeheartedly agree with.** What we disagree with is the twisting and misapplication of that principle and the fact they've highjacked it from the Bible.

BIBLE REF.
Psalm 111:10
Proverbs 1:7
Romans 1:18–20
Romans 2:14–16
Colossians 2:3

It's true for any topic. From the secular perspective, why fight for:	
Abortion?	Women are equal, to be valued and respected.
Euthanasia?	Humans are worthy of dignity and mercy.
Social justice?	Justice is good and right.
LGBTQ+ rights?	All humans deserve care, love, and fair treatment.
Environmentalism?	The earth is to be valued and stewarded well.

But again, if the universe is a cosmic accident with no absolute or eternal purpose, why care about any of these things? **The core principles that fuel secular passion are all things Christians approve of because they all come from, and only from, the Bible!**

Showing the secularist where we agree and that he has good reason to be passionate for a particular principle is a powerful argument against secularism and for biblical truth. **It demonstrates to the nonbeliever that the principle they love does exist but only because it comes from God.** He made it and defines it and it's only rightly realized within a biblical framework. Their worldview has no rational basis for the value they adore.

The unbeliever's awareness of a truth, misapplied as it

may be, **shows the morality and conscience given them by their Creator, whose image they reflect.** The effects of the Fall are also on display as the unbeliever attempts to twist what is good for their own sinful purposes.

As God's image bearers, every human has the truthfulness of the biblical worldview written on their hearts and hears the unceasing testimony of creation and conscience. Ultimately, the reason the nonbeliever doesn't make the connection of his passion to the Bible is because he doesn't want to (Romans 1:18–20, 2:14–16).

Although the secularist's worldview can't account for the real thing he loves, the Bible can. **The good thing that resonates with him does exist. Just not in his worldview and not for his purpose.** It exists in the only true reality, God's reality. The nonbeliever either needs to stop stealing from the biblical worldview or get saved. We're praying for the latter!

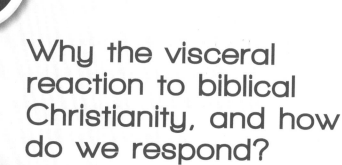

Why the visceral reaction to biblical Christianity, and how do we respond?

Christianity is the most persecuted religion in the world, and hostility toward Christians in the west seems to be growing exponentially. Why?

In short, darkness hates light. The battle raging today and throughout history is ultimately a war between the only two foundational worldviews. One worldview is built on the light of the truth of God's Word and the other is mired in the darkness of man's ideas and the Enemy's lies. It's the same battle of God's Word versus man's — as old as Genesis 3.

Christians must realize that as we stand on Scripture, defend the faith, and proclaim the gospel, we're simultaneously attacking the nonbeliever's worldview. Again, neutrality doesn't exist. **By proclaiming God's Word as true, we're declaring their foundation false. And by attacking their foundation, we're shaking the entire edifice of their worldview.** How they think, live, justify, argue, make choices, cope with the past, find meaning in the present, or plan for the future are all part of the edifice of their worldview that collapses if their foundation falls. **In other words, as their foundation crumbles, so does their identity. No wonder they zealously and emotively defend it as if their lives depended on it. In a sense, it does.**

As our culture, and much of the church, turns away from the anchor of God's absolute truth, the secular view of truth as fluid, personal, and defined by feelings dominates (just as

BIBLE REF.
Genesis 3
Jeremiah 9:6
John 3:19–20
John 15:18–24
1 Peter 3:15
2 Timothy 2:24–25
1 John 3:13

portrayed in Genesis 3:6). This has resulted in people feeling increasingly free to simply emotively attack what they view as a danger to the definition of their being. This is why unbelievers are so emotional and frequently illogical and irrational as they attack Christianity.

With this in mind, how do we respond? The way the Bible tells us to. We speak truth in love. **We uncompromisingly defend the faith with gentleness and respect with the hope of salvation for a lost soul, not to win a debate or vindicate ourselves** (1 Peter 3:15; 2 Timothy 2:24–25). Every conversation, Facebook post, and tweet are to be saturated in this disposition out of love for people, love for God, by God's command, and for His glory.

Being bold and standing firm on God's Word does not mean being disrespectfully brash or harsh. The Gospel of Jesus Christ is offensive enough to unbelievers on its own. It doesn't need our help. It's been said, "You don't cut off someone's nose and then give them a rose to smell."

Christians are to give a defense, without being defensive. We should have such confidence in God and the truthfulness of His Word that we are not intimidated, scared, or offended when someone disagrees, no matter how passionate they are. It's true whether they believe it or not. We lovingly share that truth and pray they believe because eternity is at stake, not because we want to be seen as right.

Let us remember that we do God's will God's way, or we're not really doing His will.

A lesson from Rehoboam for Christians today

In 1 Kings 12, Solomon's son Rehoboam becomes king. The people of Israel tell Rehoboam they'll gladly serve him if he lightens the workload Solomon had placed on them. Rehoboam says return in three days and we'll talk. During those three days Rehoboam gets council first from the older advisors of his father and then from his friends. The older advisors say listen to the people and his friends say to tell the people he's "the man" and will be tougher than his father. Rehoboam gladly listens to his friends, the people reject him as king, and the kingdom splits.

Reading the account, it's apparent Rehoboam didn't value the advice of the elder advisors. So why talk to them at all? It would seem because that's what he's expected to procedurally do as a new king. It's what he's supposed to do, so that's what he does. But as soon as he "checks the box" and hears advice he's not a fan of, he immediately goes to those who will tell him what he wants to hear and probably was already thinking.

Here's the connection. How often do we as Christians treat the Bible the way Rehoboam treated the elder advisors? We have or are asked a question about origins, morality, sexuality, marriage, gender, salvation, etc. And we may initially go to the Bible for an answer because that's what Christians are supposed to do. We check the box. **Yet as soon as the Bible's answer isn't what we expected or wanted — or seems too controversial — we close that "outdated" book and quickly seek the advice of our peers,**

BIBLE REF.
1 Kings 12
Jeremiah 23:29, 29:11
Matthew 19:4–5
2 Corinthians 10:5
Colossians 4:6
2 Timothy 2:24–25
Hebrews 4:12
Jude 1:3

friends, and culture — those around us whose ideas are modern, less combative (or in agreement) with the culture, and probably in line with what we're already thinking.

Of course, this is exactly how Christians are NOT to treat Scripture. God's Word is not a buffet: "I'll have some of John 3:16 and Jeremiah 29:11 (typically out of context) but will pass on Genesis 1–11 and Matthew 19:4–5." The Word of God is not optional, it's the absolute authority and truth for every topic! Either we bow and submit to what the Bible says on any given issue or we are in rebellion against it.

Let's not be like Rehoboam, who went to the elders to just "check the box." **Let's be sure we're training ourselves and those under our care to sincerely seek answers from God's Word as the final authority.**

Whether we intuitively like what it says or not, we make every thought bow to Scripture and obey Christ the King (2 Corinthians 10:5).

When Christians do this, it's then, and only then, that we have powerful answers to today's scientific and moral questions. By unleashing the truthfulness and authority of all of God's Word, we demolish arguments raised against God's knowledge, effectively contend for the faith, encourage the believer, challenge the skeptic, and clear a path for the gospel (Jude 1:3; 2 Timothy 2:24–25; Colossians 4:6).

Christianity is just like all other religions, right?

It's been said that all religions are the same and only seemingly different. In truth, Christianity is profoundly different from every religion with only superficial similarities.

Every other religion, including atheism — a religion by definition[1] — basically says you can save yourself. Do enough good deeds to please a god, gods, force, or yourself, and you can earn salvation (for atheists, satisfaction). **The Bible emphatically teaches the opposite. No one can earn salvation because God's standard is perfection.** Even our good works are saturated with our sin and are filthy rags before a holy God (Isaiah 64:6).

To earn salvation, we'd have to live a life of perfect obedience to all of God's laws (James 2:10). And since God sees our motives and thoughts, those must always be perfectly pure and God exalting (Matthew 5:21–30). Of course, none can do this and thus Scripture says, "All have sinned and fall short of the glory of God" (Romans 3:23).

We also cannot comprehend the gravity of our sin because we cannot fathom the holiness, justice, and infinite nature of the God we've sinned against. Think of it this way — lie to a child and there are limited consequences; lie to a spouse and the consequences increase; lie to the government and jail awaits. Same sin, different consequences because of whom the

1 A definition for religion from Merriam-Webster Dictionary: "a cause, principle, or system of beliefs held to with ardor and faith."

sin is against. And every sin is an act of treason against the sovereign of the universe, whom we're attempting to supplant with ourselves. **Like Adam and Eve, just one sin justifies our separation from a perfect God who won't tolerate any sin in His holy presence.** Consequently, mankind is hopeless on his own and requires the intervention of a Savior.

All other religions are man grasping for truth and salvation. The Hindu Vedas say truth is mysterious, Buddha searched for truth, and Muhammad said he pointed to the truth. **However, Jesus said, "I am the way, and the truth, and the life; no one comes to the Father but through Me" (John 14:6, NASB).** Jesus isn't "a way" and doesn't "point" to the truth; He is the truth and only way to heaven. Jesus is God become flesh, a fact He continually declared and demonstrated by forgiving sins and performing miracles (Mark 2:1–12). He came from heaven to become our blood relative, to do for us what we could never do for ourselves. Christianity is God reaching to man.

Jesus, the Last Adam, lived a perfect life, died on the Cross to pay the perfect infinite price we couldn't pay, and defeated death by rising from the grave. **No other religion has an empty tomb!** Every other major religious leader is dead. Only Jesus rose from the grave, the ultimate confirmation of who He is and what He taught (Acts 2:23–24); that all who will repent (turn away from) their sin and put their faith solely in Christ will be saved (John 6:29; Acts 4:12).

No, Christianity isn't like other religions. Man's word and religions say do; God's Word in Christianity says done in Christ. Whose word will you trust?

More Answers

Find additional information on the topics in this book with *The New Answers Book* series, the *Answers Book 4 Teens* series, and *One Race, One Blood Revised & Updated*, all from Master Books:

Page 10 – "You fool"
The New Answers Book 2; Introduction, Why Is the Christian Worldview Collapsing in America?

Page 12 – Only two?
Answers Book 4 Teens, Volume 1; Q13, How can we be sure Jesus is the only way to get to God?

Page 14 – The neutrality myth
The New Answers Book 3; Chapter 35, Wasn't the Bible Written by Mere Men?

Page 16 – Be "tolerant" or else
The New Answers Book 4; Chapter 22, What Are the Tactics of the New Atheists?

Page 18 – The Genesis connection
The New Answers Book 3; Chapter 8, Did Bible Authors Believe in a Literal Genesis?

Page 20 – How can you believe the Bible?
The New Answers Book 3; Chapter 35, Wasn't the Bible Written by Mere Men?

Page 24 – What's the biblical response to abortion?
Answers Book 4 Teens, Volume 2; Q13, What about abortion, cloning, and stem cells? At school I'm taught that these things are good for society!

Page 26 – Isn't abortion a woman's legal right and choice?
The New Answers Book 3; Chapter 17, What About Eugenics and Planned Parenthood?

Page 28 – Isn't it just a fetus, unviable outside the womb?
The New Answers Book 2; Chapter 29, When Does Life Begin?

Page 30 – Shouldn't people have the right to die?
The New Answers Book 3; Chapter 17, What About Eugenics and Planned Parenthood?

Page 32 – What about cloning?
Answers Book 4 Teens, Volume 2; Q13, What about abortion, cloning, and stem cells? At school I'm taught that these things are good for society!

Page 34 – What's the big deal with stem cells?
The New Answers Book 3; Chapter 14, What About Cloning and Stem Cells?

Page 38 – The biblical answer to racism
One Race, One Blood; Chapter 5, One Blood

Page 40 – What about "interracial" marriage?
One Race, One Blood; Chapter 6, One Flesh

Page 42 – Doesn't the Bible condone slavery?
The New Answers Book 3; Chapter 33, Doesn't the Bible Support Slavery?

Page 44 – Isn't the Bible sexist?
Answersingenesis.org; Inferior or Equal by Becky Stelzer

Page 46 – What's the biblical take on feminism?
Answersingenesis.org; Feminism by Steve Golden

Page 48 – Are social justice and intersectionality part of the Gospel?
One Race, One Blood; Chapter 2, A Bridge Too Far

Page 50 – What about the inequality of genocide?
Answersingenesis.org; Good Without God? by Dr. Elizabeth Mitchell

Page 54 – What's the origin and definition of marriage?
Answersingenesis.org; What's Behind Today's Attacks on Marriage? by Bryan Osborne

A QUICK, CONCISE, AND EASY-TO-READ BOOK OF ANSWERS!

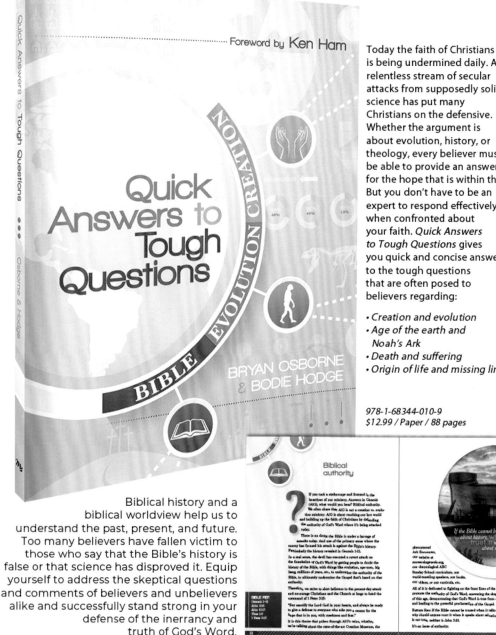

Foreword by Ken Ham

Today the faith of Christians is being undermined daily. A relentless stream of secular attacks from supposedly solid science has put many Christians on the defensive. Whether the argument is about evolution, history, or theology, every believer must be able to provide an answer for the hope that is within them. But you don't have to be an expert to respond effectively when confronted about your faith. *Quick Answers to Tough Questions* gives you quick and concise answers to the tough questions that are often posed to believers regarding:

- *Creation and evolution*
- *Age of the earth and Noah's Ark*
- *Death and suffering*
- *Origin of life and missing links.*

978-1-68344-010-9
$12.99 / Paper / 88 pages

Biblical history and a biblical worldview help us to understand the past, present, and future. Too many believers have fallen victim to those who say that the Bible's history is false or that science has disproved it. Equip yourself to address the skeptical questions and comments of believers and unbelievers alike and successfully stand strong in your defense of the inerrancy and truth of God's Word.